Reported Killed *in* Action

Reported Killed *in* Action

an unexpected soldier,
a remarkable life

LISA BEICHL

Deeds Publishing

Published by Deeds Publishing in Athens, GA
www.deedspublishing.com

Printed in The United States of America

Library of Congress Cataloging-in-Publications Data is available upon request.

ISBN 978-1-944193-04-1

Cover design and layout by Mark Babcock

Photography by Melissa Kelly, www.melissakelly.com

Books are available in quantity for promotional or premium use. For information, email info@deedspublishing.com.

First Edition, 2015

10 9 8 7 6 5 4 3 2 1

A.M.D.G.
and to Mom and Dad

Contents

Acknowledgements

MANY INDIVIDUALS AND GROUPS HELPED MY DAD IMMENSELY TOWARDS THE end of his life and we are thankful. From Donna, Val and Gloria of the Visiting Angels, under Connie Glynn's leadership; Lashay of Liberty In-Home Care and Noel; Pat Owen, CRNP, his geriatric Nurse Practitioner at the VA; to the Hospice nurses from Life Choice. Also a special thank you for the amazing care he received at the Hospice and Palliative Care Unit of the Community Living Center (Veterans Administration) in Philadelphia skillfully led by Kim Woon-Ok, CRNP, including the nurses Shirlene, Jennine, Katrina, Kimerly, Ameika, Joycette, Dominique, Cheryl, Milayne, Alex, Julia, and Lourdes, our social worker Stephanie, and Betty Ann, Deborah, Chaplain Fredi and anyone else I forgot, thank you. To all the patients in the VA hospice unit past and present, especially Mr. Tommy Pembroke (RIP). Special thanks to Linda Frangipane-Simon of Life Choice's Veterans unit, without whom we would never have met Scott—very special thanks to Scott C. Brown, Director Veterans Advisory Commission (Philadelphia and Delaware County) for taking my dad out many times when I was just too tired, for helping me navigate the complexities of hospice care, for continuing to say the rosary, and for getting my dad's war efforts recognized.

Thank you to all our friends (especially from the German Society—including the Women's Auxiliary, the Zither Ensemble—in particular Kurt and Rita Maute and the Zapf Family, and St. Joe's Chemistry Department) and to neighbors in Overbrook and friends, especially Darlene Quinn, Regina and Thomas Engelhardt, Terri Bassitt, Jeanna Holtz, Elizabeth Hagan Borst, Dr. Robin Hornstein, and Suzy Chesny, who provided great encouragement.

Thanks to Brad Herron and Pennsylvania Congressman Bob Brady for getting my dad's POW status reinstated in 2011.

Thank you Rev William J. Byron, S.J. for coming to our house to hear my dad's Confessions, give him Holy Communion, as well as provide Anointing of the Sick (on many occasions).

Thank you Rev. George Bur S.J., William H McGarvey Jr., Patricia McGarvey Knebels, Bill Avington, and the St. Joseph's Prep Alumni Association (President Ed Foy) for allowing my dad's memory to continue through awarding him the "Alumnus of the Year Award 2014-2015."

Many thanks to all those who helped by reading versions of the book or offering suggestions, including my mom, Isabella, and my sisters, Isabel, Karen, and Chris (who unexpectedly found the 1939 diary), nieces Necie and Chrissy and nephew Sean, and especially my brother-in-law Francis who helped reorganize the content. Special thanks and appreciation to Andy Waskie, PhD for historical context, Sherrie Dulworth for her edits, Christel Tillmann for her input including translation assistance in editing the German articles and letters, Karin Rosnizeck for her help translating and linking cultural issues, and especially Marco Padovani for graciously stepping in late in the game with excellent structural, editing and historical suggestions and Doris Simon, not only for her significant editing, research and translation assistance (especially with the 1939 Diary), for helpful explanations regarding historical context, and for understanding my dad so well.

Special thanks to Mark Babcock for the outstanding layout and design, to Melissa Kelly for the amazing photography, to Braelen Hill of the National Infantry Foundation for the photos at Fort Benning, and to Bob Babcock, President, Historian and Archivist of the Army's 4th Infantry Division Organization, whose painstaking work in retrieving and archiving the After Action Reports (AAR) during the Division's WWII experience lent important detail to the history. Thanks to Robert S. Rush, PhD, Historian to the Office of the Surgeon General of the Army. And sincere gratitude to all the men of the 4th Infantry past and present (Steadfast and Loyal), to all those who fought, were wounded or killed in battle, and to all the scientists whose work on the Manhattan Project provided an ultimate end to the war.

Preface

IF YOU'RE READING THIS BOOK, YOU MAY KNOW SOMETHING ABOUT MY dad, George Beichl. He is probably best known for his tenure as Chair of the Chemistry Department at St Joseph's University in Philadelphia or perhaps for his work as the President of the German Society of Pennsylvania. You may know him as a faithful parishioner who attended daily Mass at Our Lady of Lourdes Catholic Church in Overbrook. Still others may have read his "Letters to the Editor" in newspapers and journals on many topics including education, Catholic or German-American issues.

But to me he was Dad. He often wrote me letters and encouraged me to write my own. He gave me things to think about, challenged my perspectives on issues, encouraged me to see the good in all people and situations, stressed the importance of forgiveness, and tried to get me to "take it easy."

In 2007 I moved back to Philadelphia to care for my parents, then in their late 80's. I was moving from a fast-paced life. I had lived in Germany for a number of years working in international health insurance and was fortunate to have been able to travel the globe in that function. Returning to Philadelphia to care for my parents was a major adjustment. So while I expected life to be a little complicated, I had no idea that I would end up unearthing a piece of history in the process.

Dad's journey ended in 2015 with his death, but the amazing, inspiring, and untold story of his earlier life now becomes its own new chapter in his legacy. This book tells of my father's extraordinary resilience and enjoyment of life in the face of some steep tribulations. I wanted to share this tribute with others; some who were fortunate enough to know him and others whom I hope will feel like they did.

Introduction

FOR AS LONG AS I CAN REMEMBER, MY DAD WANTED TO WRITE A BOOK.

I heard a lot about this book. When I was in high school he was going to write "Ancient Greek for Businessmen," which I didn't take seriously, then I learned he was a distinguished student of ancient Greek and was indeed serious. In 1986 he actually did write a book, *Problem Solving Techniques in Chemistry*, a work that details the unit basis method of problem solving. He worked tirelessly to get it published. When he was in his 90's, I drove him to a meeting of the American Chemical Society in Philadelphia to generate interest. Initially I was annoyed that he wanted me to find a way to get him to the Convention Center in downtown Philly—could I get off from work? Could I park close enough to the entrance so he would make it? This little expedition would be a challenge given his physical health. I worried how he would scale the giant floors without falling down or suffering from a heart attack. Even worse, he did not register for the event:

"I am an Emeritus member," he said.

"You need proof!" I replied.

We somehow managed—*notice they gave him a plastic badge holder, without a badge in it!* It seemed that his gigantic walker, white hair, and suit sufficed as evidence of his Emeritus status.

While the publishers that we met were very kind, there was still "no dice" on the publication. Even his next door neighbor, Maya, lent a hand with ideas and suggestions regarding potential publishers. It seemed that no one was interested in publishing this academic method that he taught at Saint Joseph's University for 50 years. In fact, he, as Chair of the Chemistry Department, required his professors to teach this method to the collective thousands of students who went on to excel in their chosen careers as scientists, nurses, and doctors. I found it was heartbreaking that no one was interested.

In addition to his work as a professor, he was also an activist for education, all things Catholic, as well as German causes. To this end, he received many awards over his lifetime. These serve in testament to his hard work and include the National Science Foundation Faculty Fellowship Award and the Lindback Award for Distinguished Teaching (the first year it was awarded). He was also recognized by the Federal German government as the recipient of the Officers Cross of the Order of Merit (das Verdienstkreuz) in 1977 as well as the Commander's Cross[1] (das Grosse Verdienstkreuz) in 1983, the same year he was awarded the Founders Medal of the German Society of Pennsylvania.

With this history it might surprise you to know that before all of these accomplishments, my dad lived through some thorny circumstances. He visited Nazi Germany as a student in 1939 before World War II (WWII), and had the misfortune of being stranded in Munich when Germany declared war. Then in 1944, well into WWII, and in spite of being the only child of a widowed (Austrian) mother (he was initially deferred military service), having a Master's degree in Chemistry (recognizing the need for chemists in the Army at that time), and having severe astigmatism and very poor eyesight, he returned to Europe as US Army Private Beichl, a soldier in the 4th Infantry Division, sent to fight against the Germans. He was captured after the infamous Battle of the Bulge

(Ardennes Offensive) and was reported as killed in action while he was held as a Prisoner of War (POW).

Returning stateside, he finally received full government clearance and completed his Army tenure as a chemist on the Manhattan Project (building the atomic bomb). Eventually he returned to the University of Pennsylvania to complete his Ph.D. in Chemistry and began a full-time career in education.

As he grew older, Dad relied on the Veterans Hospital for some of his more complicated healthcare issues. He formed a friendship with his Geriatric Nurse Practitioner at the VA, Pat, who was a big help to me as my dad's care needs increased over time. Despite the vulnerable and personal nature of these geriatric patient visits, my dad kept on pitch. Always the marketer, he persuaded Pat to attend the annual German Society *Christkindlmarkt* (Christmas Bazaar), which she continues to attend as a tradition with her daughter.

Although life was not picture perfect, we got into a groove of sorts. I was working, had home care to help out, and even was able to finance some much-needed repairs on the big 100-year-old house in Overbrook.

Then in December 2010, after all these years of care and assistance from the VA, Dad received a letter stating that his veteran's status was now Priority Group 5 and not Priority Group 3.

"Who cares?" I thought.

But my dad kept telling me, "I'm Priority Group 3, I was a POW."

He was right to be concerned.

The next letter from the VA stated that since my dad had been deemed Priority Group 5 (indicating he had served in the military), and *not* Priority Group 3 (POW status), he would have to *repay* all those years of copayments that were initially waived unless he could prove that he was a POW in Germany during WWII.

What?!

Of course he was a POW and we had the obituary from 1945 to prove it!

My calls to the VA left me shocked, shaken, and worried. I explained that Dad had been Priority 3 for *decades*, and that this was an administrative error. No one at the VA, it seemed, could help.

BEICHL

Private First Class George J. Beichl, on military leave from St. Joseph's College where he was a professor of chemistry, was killed in Germany on February 8 while serving with an infantry outfit.

Only son of Mrs. Louisa Beichl, a widow, of 1430 N. Dover st., Private Beichl entered the Army last August and had been overseas only a short time.

He was graduated from St. Joseph's High School in 1935 and from St. Joseph's College four years later. After obtaining his master degree in chemistry from the University of Pennsylvania, he did other post-graduate work at the University of Munich.

Like Dad once was, his paperwork was now "missing in action." Locating his original records would be impossible—a 1973 fire at the National Personnel Records Center in Missouri destroyed an estimated 16-18 million Official Military Personnel Files.[2] Thus began the Herculean challenge of putting together the documents to prove that Dad had served in the 4th Infantry Division in Germany, supported the Battle of the Bulge, was captured and held as a Prisoner of War (POW) at Stalag XIIA in Limburg. This was a long process and required the help of our Congressman, Bob Brady, and his VA liaison based in Port Richmond, Brad Herron.

As evidence of his POW history, I recalled my Mom talking about a diary that Dad kept where he wrote about his experiences as a prisoner. Dad was a very private man, so I had neither seen nor read the diary that lived in the top drawer of the big metal desk in his study.

So with this potential *financial disaster* looming, I asked my dad if I might read the diary.

Surprisingly, he acquiesced.

I imagined a small notebook with frayed edges; containing details of his emotional turmoil as a US soldier potentially fighting and killing his relatives still living in Germany, maybe even meeting fictional characters like Colonel Klink and Sergeant Schultz of *Hogan's Heroes* fame.

As it turned out, the "diary" was faded words scribbled in pencil around the edges of the text of a German book. A sympathetic prison guard had given Dad the book and he used it to record what he experienced. As I carefully read the yellowed and fraying pages, my shock turned to deep appreciation—it became very clear to me that the book my dad was going to write had already been written, deep in a bitter cold and damp German winter with fellow soldiers all praying to leave the harsh reality of a world at war behind them. Perhaps the biggest surprise for me was the absence of indignation or anger. Despite experiencing the deepest, most tragic time of his life, Dad managed to find joy, friendship, forgiveness, music, and an undeniable curiosity and interest to learn.

Then, three months *after* his death, to our complete surprise we found *another* diary, predating the one from his POW days.

We had known that Dad visited his family in Munich in the summer of 1939 (he convinced his mother to cash in her life insurance policy to pay for the ship's passage so he could meet his relatives), but he never mentioned a diary. It sat hidden in a faded green folder in the filing cabinet in his office next to old taxes and water bills. His words, written with a fountain pen, include vibrant descriptions of a young man discovering a new country, and experiencing the culture of a changing and sometimes frightening world. Here in the most exciting, adventurous time of his very young life, he *also* found joy, friendship, forgiveness, music, and an undeniable curiosity and interest to learn. Whether life events were difficult or smooth, my dad always seemed to have the same outcome.

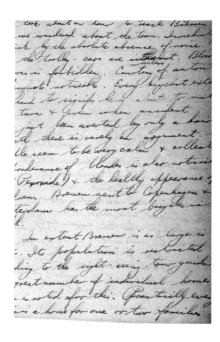

From a historical perspective, these two diaries show us very different faces of Germany through the eyes of a young American, first in 1939 and later in 1945. But contemplating the entries in both diaries, Dad's core attributes of faith in the Lord and living in the moment remain constant. When many German Americans felt pain and confusion with the rise of the National Socialists and the growing enemy status between Germans and Americans, these did not seem to influence Dad's perception. He was American to the core, and yet he deeply appreciated his German roots without conflict. He led his life as he always had, with optimism and deliberation.

But is a story about an American of German-Austrian descent living as a student in Munich in 1939 and as a POW in Wittlich and Limburg in 1945 of great consequence today? It is and for a number of reasons.

The 1939 diary adds context to the general naïveté of many Americans and Germans during the rise of National Socialism (Nazism). And through his later experience as a POW in WWII Germany, he watches as the country moves from a position of confident strength to dejected resignation, eventually watching them surrender by waving white flags.

The interplay of a "pro-German American" sent to fight against the "Germans" lends a unique perspective to history. And the significance is more than historical, it's also contemporary. When we reflect upon the Iraq War and the subsequent questioning of the patriotism of Muslims in America, it seems eerily familiar to the mistaken belief in the 1930s and 1940s that all Germans sympathized with the Nazis. If history repeats itself, we are wise to read the words of this young man and see the world through his eyes.

This story has been a very difficult one for me to tell because of the genocide and other horrors committed against the Jewish community in Europe. How could I write about a German American's experience and not feature the Jewish genocide? Even worse, how could I be sympathetic to the Germans when I considered the intense hatred, prejudice, and judgments against the Jews, gypsies, mentally ill, and conscientious objectors?

While there were individuals who spoke out against National Socialism and even tried to assassinate Hitler, the power of the Nazis continued to grow. Georg Elser, for example, built a bomb on his own and on November 8, 1939 attempted to assassinate Hitler (who left the meeting much earlier than usual and thus was spared).[3] Elser was shot to death in the Dachau concentration camp outside of Munich in 1945. Father Rupert Mayer, a German Jesuit priest, was a leading Catholic figure of resistance to Nazism in Munich. Though he was banned from speaking, he continued to raise his voice in opposition to National Socialism. His protests against the Nazis landed him in prison several times and also in the Sachsenhausen Concentration Camp. Then there were groups like the White Rose movement, a group of Munich University students and a professor who were arrested by the Gestapo, tried for treason and executed in 1943 for speaking out against Nazism. Why didn't any of these oppositions become a foundation to change the course of history?

My dad and I often talked about this. He fully agreed that the doctrine of National Socialism, including the treatment of the European Jewish community, was horrifying and wrong on every level. I asked him if he knew about the concentration camps when he was a POW in Germany and he said no. The only hint he recalled was that at one point when life in Stalag XIIA was very bad, one of the guards responded to his complaints by stating, "It's worse for the Jews than it is for you." While he was a prisoner he did not know how insanely inadequate the phrase "worse for the Jews than it is for you" would turn out to be.

I cried when I watched documentaries about WWII with my dad. As we talked, he reminded me that good and evil exist in the world and that in spite of the horrors committed, there were good Germans. His prison guard was a German soldier who had returned from the Russian front due to injuries. He risked his life to nurse my dad (who was considered a traitor in Germany) back to health. My dad's experiences also tell us something about shaping our national identity. He believed it was less about constricting a culture and much more about blending the positive attributes of a culture into the American experience. Perhaps the next time we see an American-Muslim woman in a hijab[4] boarding a plane with us to Chicago, we will remember that not all people who closely associate with their culture are anathema to the US. And we may remember my dad's advice that if the goal is to create a stronger America, the cultures must weave themselves into the American fabric.

While it's fascinating to see the world unfold through my dad's diaries, first in 1939 and again in 1945, it's also remarkable that after WWII, he spent his life focused on his faith, raising a family, teaching chemistry at "The College" (St. Joe's) and working diligently to repair the fractured relationship between Germany and the US. This in spite of the difficulty he had getting security clearance from the US government to work on the Manhattan Project due to his German background (was this why they put him in the Infantry in the first place?). It didn't matter. He lived in the present. He was grateful to be alive, to be back in Philadelphia working, enjoying his family and friends, and diving back in to the German culture he loved.

He was the most contented person I have ever known.

So to take us on this journey, this book is separated into two sections:

The Diaries begins with my dad's induction into the Army as a "Replacement" troop after D-Day. We then trace the steps that led him to the Infantry, starting in Brewerytown. He wrote many essays on yellow pads of paper about growing up in Philadelphia, of the Fairmount Liedertafel and Sängerfests (German choral concerts), and of the presence of National Socialism in Philadelphia. Many of the stories he told us over the years are also incorporated. This section includes his 1939 diary as a student in Munich, the 1945 diary as a POW, first in Wittlich and then in Stalag XIIA in Limburg, as well as his time on the Manhattan Project.

Giving Back summarizes the fruit his life bore, his guiding nature as a father, his work as a professor, and his efforts to improve the relationship between Germany and the US. His strong faith enabled him to ignore any biases against his German background, and to jump into life full of optimism, confidence and love. And so we meet a man as he lives to the ripe age of 96-and-a-half, who consistently lived in the present, displayed gratitude and appreciation for his life, family and friends, and remained steadfast in his Roman Catholic faith.

In telling this story I used my dad's own words as often as possible, weaving in my observations or conversations with him only to clarify context.

And I think you will agree with me, he truly had a remarkable life.

—Lisa Beichl

The Diaries:
WWII, Growing Up,
Munich and WWII

1. The Battle Of The Bulge
And The Need For Replacement Troops

WWII BEGAN IN SEPTEMBER 1939 WITH ADOLF HITLER'S INVASION OF PO-land. The war dragged on for six long years until the final Allied defeat of Nazi Germany and Japan with the atomic bomb in August 1945.[5]

One of the most important battles, the Invasion of Normandy (D-Day), occurred on June 6, 1944. It resulted in significant casualties. And though many believed this battle marked an important turning point of the war, the US Army still had to replenish troops.

An increase to the draft was urgently required, and that meant tapping into "Replacement" troops, the men that the US Army thought it would never need. Several months later, when WWII looked like it was moving to a strong finish with an Allied victory, the Germans launched a surprise counteroffensive in the Ardennes region of Belgium that shocked the world. On December 16, 1944, six months after D-Day, in the midst of a cold and dreary winter, Germany began the historic battle intended to destroy the Allied Forces forever.[6] This battle was known as the Battle of the Bulge.

The attack caught the Allies completely off guard and brought with it incredible casualties, adding immeasurable stress to the already stretched Allied troops. Unfortunately, the United States bore the brunt of the attack. In fact, the losses for the United States were so high that the training of many "Replacement" soldiers was cut short, as their presence in Europe was sorely needed.

This is how a 26-year-old man from Philadelphia, chemistry professor at St. Joseph's College, working towards his PhD in chemistry at the University of Pennsylvania—an important subject for US defense—and the only child and sole support of his widowed mother, was drafted in July 1944 and sent to support the Battle of the Bulge troops.

SAINT JOSEPH'S COLLEGE
PHILADELPHIA

OFFICE OF THE PRESIDENT

August the eighth, 1944.

Dear George,

It is a matter of very sincere regret to me that I must see you leave the College which practically since my coming here five years ago, you have served so well. The circumstances which cause your departure are not of our making and we can only hope and pray that your absence will be but a temporary one.

I shall not be here to welcome you on your return but feel that no matter how long or short the interval, the officials of the College will be as happy to welcome you back as I am regretful of your departure.

With you goes my blessing and the fervent prayer that God may return you safely and soon to the work for which I feel you are so eminently fitted.

Very sincerely yours,

Thomas J. Love SJ

President.

Mr. George J. Beichl,
c/o St. Joseph's College,
54 and City Line,
Philadelphia, Pennsylvania.

COLUMBIA UNIVERSITY
DIVISION OF WAR RESEARCH
S A M   LABORATORIES

August 17, 1944

REPLY TO PERSONNEL DEPT.

SAM LABORATORIES

3290 BROADWAY
NEW YORK 27, N. Y.
EDGECOMBE 4-4300

Private George J. Beichl
ASN #33814760
A.S.F. Reception Center,
Area #3, Bldg. #10
New Cumberland, Pa.

Dear Mr. Beichl:

Your name has been suggested to us by Dr. Martin Kilpatrick as a candidate for assignment to this project on active duty from the Army. If you are interested in this possibility, will you please fill out all the enclosed forms according to the directions attached. As soon as these forms have been returned to us, we will review them carefully in anticipation of making a request for your transfer.

Because our work is of a highly secret nature, there is very little that I can tell you about the type of work in which you might be engaged here other than to indicate that we would not request your assignment unless we felt that your training and experience could be used to good advantage.

I trust that I may have your response within the near future.

Very sincerely yours,

Ralph R. Wolf
Director of Personnel

RRW:t
Encl.

Because he was pursuing his PhD in Chemistry at the time, his advisor at the University of Pennsylvania tried to get him assigned to the Manhattan Project (atomic bomb).

FROM A YELLOW PAD OF PAPER—In fact Dr. Martin Kilpatrick who taught Physical Chemistry at the University of Pennsylvania went to Columbia University to work on the Manhattan Project. He told me to send him my Army serial number as soon as I obtained it and he would get me on the Manhattan Project.

Unfortunately, when I received my serial number we were placed on quarantine and I could make no outside calls.

When I was able to make calls it was too late to be admitted to the Manhattan Project, because I was now a member of the IRTC Infantry Replacement Training Corps. Dr. Kilpatrick told me to contact him shortly before my IRTC cycle was completed. Here again I ran into a roadblock. Due to the Battle of the Bulge, replacements were sorely needed and our units were ordered to cut short the training cycle and get on our way to Europe.

—George Beichl

ENORMOUS CASUALTIES

During the Battle of Hürtgen Forest, the average infantry company lost 150% of its strength. Each new troop realized the odds were against survival. Many troops became prisoners or casualties of war. This is exactly what happened to that 26-year-old man.

George Beichl was assigned to E Company, 2nd Battalion, 22nd Infantry. He did not join his group until sometime after December 1, 1944. He was reported "Killed in Action" in 1945 and the 22nd Infantry still refers to him as such; the name "BEICHL" is actually etched in the monument to fallen 22nd Infantry Regiment on the Memorial Walk of Honor at Fort Benning, Georgia. This monument memorializes the 2,954 soldiers killed in the line of duty between the War of 1812 and today from that unit. Retired Lieutenant Colonel and current Congressman Steve Russell (from Oklahoma) commanded the 1st Battalion, 22nd Infantry Regiment task force responsible for the search for Saddam Hussein and was a key figure in getting the memorial established.[7] The unit has a long and impressive history of proud service to the country.

Fortunately, George was still very much alive, though in 1945 he was struggling to survive in a German Prisoner of War camp. George Beichl actually passed away on February 6, 2015; safe in a Veterans Hospice in Philadelphia. And if you study the difference in dates, he was reported Killed in Action on February 8, 1945, a full 70 years and just 2 days apart.

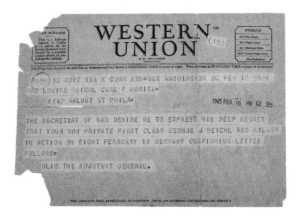

How George came to be a Prisoner of War in Germany in 1945 all began on Dover Street in a German-speaking section of Philadelphia. So, not only could he understand the harsh enemy commands and private discussions among the prison guards, but he also studied with the Germans as a student in Munich. In fact, he was in Munich when Germany attacked Poland in September 1939. And when war was declared and all German ships were needed for the war effort, George and his mother were stranded.

American prisoners captured in Ardennes in December 1944

2. The Road to Munich

HOW GEORGE HAPPENED TO BE IN MUNICH IN 1939, AND HOW HE AND his mother managed to leave once Germany declared war, all started back in Brewerytown, an ethnic working-class neighborhood in Philadelphia. George was born in Philadelphia in 1918 to a Bavarian father and an Austrian mother. This is where his values, moral compass, and appreciation of the German culture developed. To understand the impact of his experiences in Germany, it will help if you know more about the man through the many essays he wrote on yellow pads of paper.

FROM A YELLOW PAD OF PAPER—Most Americans are either immigrants or descendants of immigrants. As a result, there is a wealth of music and customs to which Americans are exposed. Unfortunately, many of the descendants of immigrants lose interest in the cultural wealth brought to America by their families and many of these cultural items die out. This is especially true if the country of origin has been an enemy of the US and engaged in warfare against it as was the case with Germany.

Unfortunately, my father (George) died of appendicitis when I was three years old. My mother (Louise) could have had a position with the family of George de Benneville Keim, President of the Reading Railroad, for whom she had worked in Europe and who brought her to Philadelphia. Neighbors suggested that she could enroll me in Girard College[8] where I would obtain a good education and learn a trade free of charge, but my father had a deathbed request not to let me be an apprentice (due to the physical and emotional mistreatment he experienced as an apprentice).

FROM A YELLOW PAD OF PAPER—She wanted to raise me and preferred to work from home. A neighbor suggested that she take in washing and offered her one of her customers. This suited my mother since it would enable her to work at home and thus see to my education. Eventually she secured washing from the Majestic Hotel which was located on Broad and Girard. There was a library behind the hotel which I would later visit and read chemistry books when I delivered the clean laundry back to the hotel.

My mother decided that she would enroll me in the St. Ludwig's parochial school which was close to our home. St. Ludwig's was a German ethnic parish which the non-German's called "Dutch Louie's." She was able to convince the pastor to enroll me at age 5, a year earlier than the traditional age 6.[9]

In addition to the regular grammar school curriculum, German language was also taught. All students learned to greet the pastor on his occasional visit to the classroom "Gelobt sei Jesus Christus, guten Morgen (Tag) Hochwürden" or Praised be Jesus Christ, good morning (afternoon) Father.

I still recall a ditty our pastor Father George Michl taught us during recess in the schoolyard. "O wie herrlich, O wie schön ist es in die Schule zu geh'n" which can be rendered into colloquial English as oh how nifty oh how cool it is for us to go to school.

My godfather Hans Karl taught me a ditty which I asked my teacher for permission to recite: "Gigerl sein, das ist fein. Jeder kann nicht Gigerl sein." To be a gigolo, that is fine. Not everyone can be a gigolo. She thought it was amusing and took me to the second grade class where I repeated it and pounded my hand on the desk for effect. Later I learned that one of the pupils told his mother, a German, "we had a French kid recite something in class today."

My godparents Hans and Therese Karl were both Bavarians. He was a native of Eslarn, my father's home town. They both saw to it that I was exposed to the Bavarian culture.

—George Beichl

He reflected on his life in Brewerytown.

FROM A YELLOW PAD OF PAPER—The German immigrants who come to our shores today are well-educated. The Germans who came years ago were primarily working class men and women but it was their dedication to their cultural heritage which preserved it in the many clubs and organizations which they founded and for which we should be grateful.

As a son of immigrants who came from Germany and Austria, I was exposed to the German culture at an early age and enjoyed it. People often ask me, "was bist Du?" or what are you? Since my father came from the Oberpfalz of Bavaria and my mother from the Austrian province of Steiermark I reply: Ich bin halber Bayer, halber Steirer, und der ganze Amerikaner. I am half Bavarian, half Styrian and entirely American.

I was born and reared in a German village in Philadelphia called Brewerytown. It extended from 26th to 33rd Street in the West and from Poplar Street to Columbia Avenue in the North. The Germans called it Brauerstadt i.e., Brewerytown for obvious reasons.

On a summer evening when the windows were open you would often hear a zither[10] being played, a piano, violin, mandolin, or accordion. You also heard more singing than is usually heard nowadays. The Fairmount Liedertafel (a German singing group in Brewerytown) had a men's chorus and a women's chorus.

The Fairmount Liedertafel's choruses offered concerts through the dreary days of Prohibition.

One of their concerts still lives in my memory. It was an informal concert held after the repeal of Prohibition in 1933. The chorus would visit different saloons to promote the resumption of beer consumption. On one evening they visited Schweizerhof's Saloon at Dover and Master Streets, which was down the street from where I lived. This was in the days before air-conditioning. The windows were open and the choral singing was a delight to hear. One of the songs in their repertoire was so beautiful that I made an effort to learn its identity. It turned out to be "Des Jägers Abschied" (The Hunter's Farewell). Not only was the melody, a piece by Mendelssohn, beautiful, but the text was equally beautiful.

"Wer hat dich du schöner Wald aufgebaut so hoch dadroben. Wohl, den Meister will ich loben solang noch mein Stimm' erschallt. Lebewohl—lebewohl du schöner Wald!"

Who built you, you beautiful forest, so high above me. Indeed that Master I will praise as long as my voice resounds. Farewell—farewell you beautiful forest!

Contrast these sublime thoughts with those of the Brewer's Union which issued miniature beer steins for one of the festivals with a caption imprinted with a parody of the well-known adage:

Hopfen und Malz (Hops and malt)
Gott erhalt's (May God preserve them)

The Socialist brewers couldn't tolerate the effrontery of the word "God" on one of their favors. Their version read:

Hopfen und Malz (Hops and malt)
Natur erhalt's (May nature preserve them)

The singing societies in Philadelphia were an important thread in the German American community, but they were often linked to political belief systems like socialism or communism. Belonging to a German singing society could be interpreted as having political leaning that was against the American grain.

FROM A YELLOW PAD OF PAPER—Most German choruses belonged to the Vereinigte Sänger (united singers). But since the founders were Brewers who were strong union men, the Fairmount Liedertafel belonged to the Arbeitergesangvereine (workers chorus). Many of the Arbeitergesangvereine sang songs that praised the workers and socialism. But there was little tendency to promote such songs by the Liedertafel, although for a Sängerfest they would sing whatever the national group prescribed.

I attended one such Sängerfest in New York, during the war, where the stage was festooned with banners supporting Stalin and naturally the US too, and calling for the defeat of Hitler.

*

In fact, it was at this Sängerfest during WWII where Fritz Kuhn spoke about the need for German Americans to support Hitler and the National Socialist cause. Kuhn held the title of "Führer" of the Deutsch-Amerikanischer Volksbund (German-American Bund).[11] In an extract from the German-American Bund pamphlet "Awake and Act" written by Kuhn in 1936:

> The Bund is American in its inception and in its field of endeavor, German in its idealism and character. To it has fallen the great task of spurring the spiritual awakening of the German element. The German-American Volksbund is inspired with the National Socialist world concept. We desire that the spirituality be transmitted to the Germans of America through mediums of flaming words and inspiring examples. We must leave nothing undone to gain access to the hearts and minds of our fellow German Americans. We will foster understanding of our homeland, convert our American fellow citizens into true friends of the present-day Germany.[12]

But when George was growing up, the German culture he experienced was much simpler. Many immigrants simply transplanted their customs into the Philadelphia soil. In a way they were living German, but in America.

FROM A YELLOW PAD OF PAPER—The Liedertafel singers also offered occasional plays which featured peasant humor. One popular play was "Herr Lehrer, ich muss mal raus" (Teacher, I have to leave the room). The schoolboys in the play were corpulent Germans dressed in sailor suits with short pants. The teacher was Jack Eisenmann whose orchestra played all the dances. His supervisor was Bill Aust, grandfather of our Willi Aust.[13]

There was another group which also offered plays at the Liedertafel. It was known as "Die Isartaler." (The people from the Isar Valley). The Isar is the river that flows through Munich. They were led by George Lofener and Otto Bichlmeier who sang and played leading roles in the play which were played and sung in the Bavarian dialect. For music, there were zithers played by Thomas Matthauser and another gentleman I cannot recall, and a bass guitar (double necked) by Sepp G'Sinn.

These plays were given in the Bavarian dialect. As one would expect, most of the brewers were Bavarian. I had the good fortune to have been taken to these plays while I was in grammar school. As a result, I learned the Bavarian dialect. Instead of "Beine" for legs, the Bavarians say "Haxen." Instead of "Hände" for hands they say "Bratzen."

The plays usually dealt with the competition of a Jäger and a Wilderer for the affections of a "fesches Dirndl" (pretty girl). I could understand what Jäger was, i.e., a hunter, but I never grasped the significance of the Wilderer, who I later learned was a poacher, one who hunted illegally.

I not only learned German from these plays, but I was exposed to Bavarian music, for the Isartaler had two zither players and a contra guitar player . This was in the days before radios were prevalent.

This picture includes a guitar, not a contra guitar, but the zither player (on the left) in this photograph was George's Uncle Sepp Bernhart, who was married to Frieda. This photo was taken in 1913 in New York, and the accompanying Tyrolian attire and beer steins set the scene. A contra guitar has a neck with six strings and a fretboard and has a second fretless fretboard with up to nine bass strings. Imagine the sight of the Austrian and German immigrants in their traditional clothing walking along the streets of New York and Philadelphia, setting down their roots.

FROM A YELLOW PAD OF PAPER—I was so impressed by the music that I looked for the opportunity to learn to play the zither. This opportunity came when Herr Leonhard Zapf arrived in Philadelphia from Bayreuth and advertised in the German paper, the Philadelphia Gazette Demokrat, "Zither lessons 10 cents." He offered the lessons in the back bedroom of his home on Ashdale Street in Olney. Shortly thereafter he opened a music store on 5th Street near Tabor Road. Round trip on the trolley was

15 cents. The route followed the #57 trolley which ran on Master and Jefferson to the #47 trolley on 5th Street. We used "Meine Methode" by Richard Grunwald as our text. There were about a dozen schoolboys and schoolgirls who sat around a table for instruction. My mother and my godparents financed my zither lessons.

The small Beichl family was quite poor. But the neighbors in Brewerytown sought opportunities to help them survive. This was, after all, a community.

FROM A YELLOW PAD OF PAPER—When I was in 8th grade, one of the local butchers, Mr. Spohrer, hired me to get the orders from his German-speaking customers on my bicycle before school and write down their orders. His son would then deliver the orders by automobile. This was back in the days when few people had telephones.

I only recall one problem. A Mrs. Kelbinger ordered "Nieren." Since I had never tasted them or even heard of them, I had to stop home to learn that they were "kidneys." Since those days I have enjoyed many tasty dinners of "Saure Nieren." (Sour Kidneys are a traditional south German dish)

Neighbors addressed each other, as well as shopkeepers, as Mr. and Mrs. and used the polite form of you, "Sie." Of course we youngsters were addressed with the familiar "Du." One day my mother returned from the store and in a shocked voice said, "Mrs. Schmitt said 'Du' to Mr. Stein." The interchange went something like this, "Stein, Du hast mir schlechte Kartoffeln verkauft." (Stein, you sold me bad potatoes.) Mrs. Schmitt was a Bavarian who had the reputation of being outspoken, or as the Germans would say, "nahm kein Blatt vor den Mund" (didn't mince words).

We Americans of German descent were called "half smokes." When a young child went to the butcher store with his mother, the butcher invariably gave him a "half-smoke" which was a hot dog.

Language issues are sure to be present with any sets of immigrants, and the Germans in Brewerytown were no exception:

FROM A YELLOW PAD OF PAPER—Children of German parents rarely spoke German outside of the home. They understood enough German to respond to "Mach die Tür zu," (close the door), "Mach die Tür auf" (open the door). They knew that Spitzbub (rascal) was not as serious an epithet as Lausbub, but German grammar sometimes infiltrated our English although we were unaware of it.

I remember asking a friend of Irish descent, "Are you coming with?" which imitates the German "Gehst mit?" He was puzzled by my question and wanted to know if he were coming with what?

German words were often used as nicknames. One fellow was known as "Schmalzie"—which is derived from the German word "Schmalz" for "lard." I eventually learned how he received this sobriquet.

Back in the 1920's if a child had an infectious disease, a representative of the City Board of Health would visit the home and place a sign on the front door identifying the infectious disease—Measles, Chicken Pox, Whooping Cough, etc.

The Board of Health agent visited this family and inquired of the mother, who could not speak English well, her son's name. She thought that he was asking how she was treating him. She told the man that she rubbed his chest with Schmalz, i.e., lard. In fact she printed out the word Schmalz. I recently learned of his true identity from his cousin Bill Glaser, a member of the German Society. Schmalzie was actually Albert Goessler.

Language problems abound when speakers fail to pronounce the words correctly. Fairly recently, my wife's cousin and her daughter visited us from Vienna. After they expressed an interest in visiting Saks Fifth Avenue Department Store, which was nearby, we promised to pick them up within an hour after they had looked at all the fashions on display. When we picked them up, they described a strange incident that had occurred. It seemed that when they were but a short distance from the store, they wanted to make sure that they were headed in the right direction. They went up to an elderly gentleman and asked him if they were on the right path for Saks. He immediately turned away from them, ignoring their question. Puzzled by this rudeness, they asked another gentleman and got the same treatment. We asked how they phrased their question. Their reply was "We are looking for Saks" but in their pronunciation it sounded like "Veer looking for Zex" which made it clear to us why both gentlemen refused to become involved.

The Germans who came here not only enriched America with their skills as brewers, bakers, butchers, tool and die makers, but they also saw to it that their cultural heritage was preserved.

It should be noted that in preserving these traditions they set a priority on first learning the language of their new Heimat (homeland). Most of them had only a Grammar School education but they attended English classes in the Evening Schools set up in the local High Schools. They also studied American history so that they could become naturalized

American citizens. There was never a need for German translators to enable German Americans to vote or pay their utility bills.

And the language also surfaced in the Philadelphia German Newspapers that kept the immigrant community abreast of community issues and events:

FROM A YELLOW PAD OF PAPER—There were two daily German newspapers published in those days, "The Philadelphia Tageblatt" which was the Union newspaper with a socialist philosophy, and the "Philadelphia Gazette Demokrat" which was later absorbed by the New Yorker Staatszeitung.[14] The latter paper had an office in the German Society with secretary Frau Schmutz of happy memory who was a voracious reader and faithful user of our Library.

Most families subscribed to one or the other of these newspapers. The editor of the Tageblatt was Louis Werner, father of Mina Werner of happy memory who was an active member of the Women's Auxiliary.[15] She recalled serving as a reporter for the Tageblatt including an article she wrote on a fire in Brewerytown.

The Tageblatt promoted pacifism in keeping with its Socialist orientation. As a result, Mr. Werner was accused of anti-Americanism during World War I and had to stand trial. Fortunately the war ended before a verdict was attained and he was exonerated.

The Gazette had a column entitled "der Flaneur" which described all the activities of the various German clubs. One of the last Flaneurs was Otto Leukert. Since this column was not retained by the Staats-Zeitung, the local German-Americans are uninformed of what is transpiring in their community.

I would browse through the Gazette Demokrat. One day there was an article that featured a criminal trial. There were so many technical terms with which I was unfamiliar, that I decided that I had better elect German as my foreign language elective in High School.

—George Beichl 2005

I think you can tell by now that George loved all things German.

FROM A YELLOW PAD OF PAPER—An alcoholic would come once or twice a year for a handout. Mrs. Wachter would make him take a bath and then would give him some of Mr. Wachter's old clothes.

Once a frequenter of the Liedertafel (a Fairmount based German singing group) complained continually about the US, and praised Germany. Mr. Wachter took a German newspaper and pointed out to the man that the liner Bremen was sailing from New York on Tuesday. "If it is so good over there why don't you take the ship over there?" There were no more comments about Germany after that.

Once Joe Wachter and Gus Derkits were candidates for the presidency of the Liedertafel. Derkits said something that displeased Wachter. He vaulted over the bar and told them to make a ring and the two engaged in fisticuffs. After the fight, both shook hands. Wachter was elected.

—George Beichl

Let's start at the beginning.

3. A Jesuit Education

READING BOOKS WAS NEAR THE TOP OF THE LIST OF GEORGE'S "FAVORITE things." He particularly enjoyed reading biographies, learning what events impacted the lives of famous men and how they overcame obstacles. And he could recall the details of these books almost verbatim. So it could not have been much of a surprise when he received a partial scholarship to a private high school, St. Joseph's Preparatory School (the Prep), conveniently located a little over one mile from his home in Brewerytown. It was at the Prep that he was exposed to the rigors of a classical education and he fell in love with Greek (three years required) and Latin (four years required).

It was also at the Prep he met many of the friends that would travel the rest of life with him. Don Cooke (also an educator who chaired the Chemistry Department at Cornell University) used to joke that George was a bit of a troublemaker in high school. He explained that at the Prep's weekly assemblies the disciplinarian would name the students who had detention that day and it went something like this: "1A: Bob Smith; 3B: Frank Jones; 4A: Fred McDonough; and *Beichl.*"

This represented quite a departure from the voracious reader.

The Prep educated a diverse student body, including some from wealthy Philadelphia and Main Line families. So when his fellow students learned that he had easy access to beer (coming from Brewerytown), he started a small business selling beer to his high school friends. In the winter he kept the beer on the rooftop to keep it cold and in the warmer months he kept the beer in his locker.

Eventually, one of the Jesuit priests discovered the commercial business enterprise and put an end to it. He was suspended for two weeks of school unless his mother came in to talk to the priests about his conduct. When his mother received the note from school, she asked George, "What should I do?" He said to do nothing and forget about it. And so she did.

He took the next two weeks off from the Prep and they deducted 15 points from every grade in every subject that semester. In spite of this, he graduated either second or third in his class. When later asked if he had not had those points deducted, would he have graduated at the top of his class, his response was, "No, the top guy was really *very* smart."

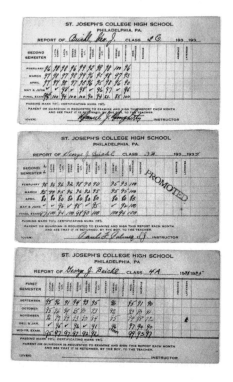

George graduated from the Prep in 1935. He explained the Nazi (National Socialist) influence in Philadelphia at that time through two stories.

While a student at the Prep, he studied German. One day he saw a Nazi paper being sold on the street; it was "Deutscher Weckruf und Beobachter" and the headline was "Schwarze Mühlmäuse in the US" which was a negative reference to the Jesuits ("black moles in the US"). He brought it to his German teacher (a Jesuit priest) to be a wise guy and pretended he didn't know what it meant, in an attempt to embarrass the priest.

The "Deutscher Weckruf und Beobachter" was the newspaper for the German American Bund (a US based Nazi Organization). The newspaper had some important advertisers, including the German Railroad Information Office, North German Lloyd, and the Hamburg-Bremen Steamship Company.[16]

An article on November 11, 1937, "For or against—but no Neutral" included this statement:

"The formula today is either actively with us—or against us. Where enlightenment has penetrated there can be no neutrality. To continue to remain neutral under those circumstances means: to assume an attitude against us, against the upright preservation of the interests of our Germandom in the U.S.A."[17]

He also related the story that he had heard from a family friend, Art Beswick, who attended a funeral in Philadelphia and observed a man dressed in a brown uniform (Nazi S.A., Sturmabteilung - Storm Detachment or Assault Division) surrounded by guards who also dressed as Nazi soldiers.

It's hard to imagine today that some Nazi supporters milled about the streets of Philadelphia in brown S.A. uniforms, but apparently they did.

Though George was aware of Nazi meetings in Philadelphia, he didn't attend any. In fact, among his papers was a leaflet from "Citizens Anti-Nazi Committee of the American League for Peace and Democracy."

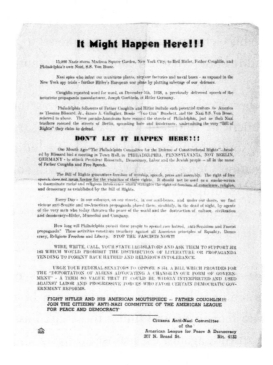

When asked about anti-Semitism in Brewerytown, he responded that he didn't see any, but that didn't mean it didn't happen.

FROM A YELLOW PAD OF PAPER—There is a semi-annual luncheon for the male residents of Brewerytown and Fairmount Sports All-timers. At one of these sessions I asked George Needleman, the son of Mr. Needleman the tailor, if he had ever experienced any anti-Semitism when he grew up in Brewerytown. He replied "absolutely not." I can honestly say that that was the impression of everyone who lived there at the time.

A second factor was that many Germans were patriotic Americans. Their children volunteered for the armed services and some stayed in the service after war. Their parents were proud of them and in our neighborhood many of the men served as air-raid wardens and auxiliary policemen. One such volunteer, Joey Wachter, made a career out of the Air Force. His father Joe Wachter, who was President of the Brewers Union, served as an auxiliary policeman.

*

Once he began his studies at St. Joseph's College (now University) in Chemistry, George intended to contribute financially to the household. Even though he was a full time college chemistry student, it was time to find a job. He heard about a position at Methodist Hospital as an orderly through another friend he made at St. Joe's College, Jack McCart—a journalism major. He worked six nights a week.

The last lab went to about 4:30 or 5:00 pm. He then took the trolley to Market Street where he got off for a spaghetti dinner that cost about 35 cents. Then he got on the El at 52nd and Market to the 15th Street car to Wolf Street (two blocks beyond Snyder Avenue), then walked to the hospital.

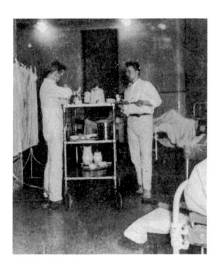

Work started at 7pm, getting patients ready for surgery. This included shaving, enemas, and catheterizations as needed. With preparations completed, they were allowed some free time for homework. They ate dinner with everyone at 11pm then George slept in a tub (they were on call all night) and Jack slept in a wheelchair. They got off at 7am and got on a trolley or streetcar to City Avenue and started the day again.

Though the work was demanding, his memories focused on the

humorous events that occurred. He smiled when he explained that in his senior year, he and Jack wanted to go to the Prom. They located a willing substitute for their shift, but were concerned that the substitute, Barney Milligan, made it to work on time. After the dance they called the Hospital to see how things went. The nurse on duty started to yell that the replacement had not shown up and that they better get down there in a hurry. They did this, but still had on their tuxedos. So when they opened the door to the pre-surgery room, one of the attendants said, "Oh look! George and Jack got married!"

And when many young men fulfilled their heavy school and work obligations at the expense of a social life, that was not the case with George. There was always time for a beer and a song. He brought many friends to their small family home on Dover Street in Brewerytown and introduced them to the songs sung at the Fairmount Liedertafel. He mentioned bringing a friend, Jack Travers, and his family to the Liedertafel for a dance including his sister and her husband (Helen and Ed Strange) and his parents, too. It's hard to imagine children bringing their parents to a dance, but that was how things were at the time. It may also be hard to believe, but the Travers lived on a houseboat in the Manayunk Canal—such modes of living on the water are no longer allowed there.

Their neighbor was a man named Tom McCormick, originally from the Fairmount section, who had a personality all his own.

One day George took a Professor from Penn, Chuck Evers, to visit the Travers. They weren't home so they then went next door to see Tom. There they drank some schnapps with him. There were a lot of flies in the place and when Evers went to swat one, Tom said, "Hey don't do that, he's one of my buddies from the war (WWI)."

At St. Joe's George was a natural leader and founded the *Royal Knights of the Keg*, mainly chemistry majors and many life-long friends, including Don Cooke (who attended both the Prep and St. Joe's College with George), and Pat Lavalle. They would take up a collection until they had enough money to buy a keg of beer. Then they might go to Bob Rowan's house (Girard Estate in South Philly), and another member, Johnny Szczepaniak, would bring lunch meat from his Dad's deli. They enjoyed their beer and sang songs. In fact they enjoyed singing the German songs so much that some of his Irish friends joined the Fairmount Liedertafel.

George settled into his German roots in Philadelphia, learned to play the zither, and sang with the Fairmount Liedertafel. He led groups of friends in beer drinking and song, worked full-time as an orderly, and studied chemistry full-time, too.

And all the while, the message of National Socialism was being spread in Philadelphia through radio broadcasts of Hitler, through meetings taking place locally, and through newspapers. And these words had impact. In fact, some German Americans were so swayed by Hitler's grand promises that they uprooted their families in Philadelphia and bought one-way ship passage back to Germany.

But there were also notable Germans who supported the US cause, including Marlene Dietrich. Dietrich contributed to the US war effort by recording anti-Nazi albums in German designed to lower the morale of German soldiers.[18] She became one of the first celebrities to raise war bonds, and she entertained US troops on the front lines. When asked why she did this she replied, "It was the decent thing to do."[19]

The genuine conflict between the beauty of the German culture and the Nazi hatred and prejudice drew lines between many German Americans. Some German-Americans preferred not to display their German culture for fear of appearing supportive of the National Socialists. Some were pained and confused by the negative and aggressive actions of the Nazis, and as we know, there were also some German Americans who believed Hitler was right. But somehow, for George, the differences were very clear. There was no conflict in appreciating the German culture while disagreeing with the Nazi worldview. His admiration of German literature and music stood in stark contrast to his disregard of the prejudice, hatred, and fear-mongering that National Socialism generated. And it made no difference to him if he attended a German singing festival in New York and a famous Nazi was speaking—right in the middle of WWII—after all, he was there to enjoy the singing, not the politics.

4. Germany in 1939 as a Student

The 1939 diary, written in both German and English, details George's encounters with the Nazis and Germans in Munich, and how he experienced National Socialism in the University. As a devout Catholic, he wrote how one professor explained that Catholicism did not reconcile with National Socialism, while another professor lauded the Catholic influence on Goethe. At the movies he watched reenactments of Hitler's *Mein Kampf* as "news reels" before the feature film. In between he talked to some Slovakian women he met at a dance, to a Dane who expressed frustration of the German position at the Scandinavian border, and to a Hungarian with Jewish roots. He asked them all of their thoughts and opinions and documented them for us to experience through him.

He also wrote about the beautiful landscape, the wonderful music, playing zither, hiking in the mountains, swimming in the lakes, visiting a myriad of museums, seeing Goethe's *Faust* performed, and deeply immersing himself in the culture that he learned to love in Philadelphia.

Knowing now what unthinkable atrocities resulted from National Socialism, it's hard to imagine how he did not see at the time how bad things would become. But he always saw the best possible outcome and so it made sense when reading his words about the anti-Semitic and anti-Catholic books being sold at the University that it was incomprehensible to him that mass extermination of Jews in Germany and Europe would result.

FROM A YELLOW PAD OF PAPER—As June 1939 approached, I was looking forward to my graduation from St. Joseph's College as a

Chemistry major and a job in the chemical industry. However, another thought came to me. Now would be the ideal time to trace my roots.

Neither my mother nor father had close relatives in America. I proposed that we visit Germany and Austria so that I could meet uncles, aunts, and cousins whom I only knew via correspondence. To cover our transportation costs, we could redeem an insurance policy. Furthermore my mother had a sister living in Munich who had invited us to spend the summer with her. With this in mind, I applied to the University of Munich for an Ausländerskurs (course for foreign students) and was accepted.

We set sail on the liner Europa of the Norddeutscher Lloyd in New York and reached our destination, Bremen. Upon our arrival, I became aware of a difference from my life in the US. My American newspapers, as well as copies of magazines such as Life, were confiscated.

—George Beichl 2005

Part 1. Arrival

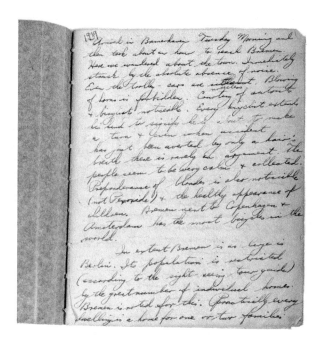

FROM THE DIARY—Arrived in Bremerhaven Tuesday morning and then took about an hour to reach Bremen. Here we wandered about the town. Immediately struck by the absolute absence of noise. Even the trolley cars were noiseless. Blowing of horns is forbidden. Courtesy of autoists and bicyclists noticeable. Every bicyclist extends his hand to signal he is about to make a turn and even when (an) accident has just been averted by only a hair's breadth there is rarely an argument. The people seem to be very calm and collected. Preponderance of blondes is also noticeable (not Peroxide) and the healthy appearance of the children. Bremen, next to Copenhagen and Amsterdam, has the most bicycles in the world.

In extent Bremen is as large as Berlin. Its population is restricted (according to the sight-seeing tour guide) by the great number of individual homes. Bremen is noted for this. Practically every dwelling is a home for one or two families.

Bremen is an old Hansa city completely surrounded by water. The toll stations are still extant where toll was formerly paid in order to gain entrance to the city.

The red roofs of Bremen are particularly striking. Quaint houses on winding streets often only one meter wide. Then to the huge Cathedral, the Bremer Dom, a massive building with wonderful artists designs. The Rathaus is also an interesting place. Its Ratskeller is noted for its good wines. Here we had a Rehragout (deer stew) with dumplings for 1.60 RM[20] in such a ration that although exceedingly hungry, my hunger was satiated. Down here the antique tables, chairs, and drawings are striking as also the huge doors with elaborate woodwork.

Ride to Munich took from 7PM to 7AM. Trains in Germany are rather old-fashioned and comfort cannot be expected for a long ride.

Once in Munich I was again attracted by the quaint houses. Red roofs, numerous flower gardens projecting from the windows. Although Munich has many apartment houses, it differs to a great extent from New York, for the Munich apartments have a friendlier appearance. My room has a veranda with countless flowers arranged about it. I am directly opposite the so-called English Garden with his Kleinhesselohersee where nightly garden concerts and strains of dance music are wafted up to my room.

The Bavarian likes color and comfort. Both of which can be seen in his clothes. The women wear Dirndl (traditional dress) decorated in variegated colors. Some with black waistcoats, red aprons, others with blue shirts, polka dot blouses, etc. The men wear shorts (leather) some brown, some black; some wear socks, some do without. Some wear gray coats with green lining, others blue coats. Some wear Tyrolian hats with feathered plumes, some bright green hats.

Here also the abundance of bicycles is noticeable. It seems to be the custom to drive the children (very young) about on bicycles by means of a basket fitted onto the handle bars. I have seen children driven in this manner by women well in their forties.

At all ages are bicycles ridden in Munich, from six to sixty years, and you can take that literally.

The cleanliness of streets is also outstanding and anyone throwing rubbish on the street must pay a fine of one Mark.

Also any pedestrian caught crossing on a red light is liable to a fine of one Mark, payable on the spot.

Königsplatz is a magnificent sight. At the farther side of the Propylaea and on the other side the New Pinakothek and the Glyptothek. In the centre is a huge square of enormous blocks. This square is only for pedestrians.

On the near side are two memorials, one on either side containing the graves of the 24 Nazis slain in 1923.[21] Before each stand two S.S. men in black garb on eternal watch, not even twitching a muscle.

The other evening we went to Trudering, a suburb of Munich. En route the landscape reminds me of New Jersey. Many small houses dot the way and all the fields have been converted into small farms. Here wheat, rye, etc. is grown. On the way we passed a construction gang exiting a building. One of the employees was a woman. Just at the time she was fetching water for the rest. The employment situation is the reverse of the American. There is definitely a labor shortage in Germany.

The Treaty of Versailles, which ended WWI, left Germany in a difficult position, having lost territory and suffering from the pressure of economic reparations. One of the reasons that Hitler was appreciated, at least in the beginning, was due to the positive impact on employment. Germany, by the late thirties, had full employment and stable prices.[22] In the US in 1939, the US was still in an economic depression.

FROM THE DIARY—In Trudering is a small summer house belonging to my cousin-in-law. It is a sturdy structure of wood painted with many hues and shades. It is of a light brown with a white border with green shutters. In the center is a brightly colored Wappenschild (coat of arms) of Munich with the Münchner Kindl drauf.[23]

In the garden various plants and vegetables are raised and in the rear there is (a) well-built bee hive and a swim basin. In the centre is a shrine to the Virgin Mary which Suckhardt described as Altbayerisch. For he said, "even though the rest of the world may think that we have lost our faith, it is still here" and he pointed to his heart. On the way home I encountered numerous men and women carrying home flowers and I began to realize more and more the sentimental nature of the Bavarians.

The other day I was also at the University. Of simple structure on the outside it is really artistically designed within. Most of the students wear leather shorts (Lederhosen) and the girls Dirndl[24] and also a great majority of the students, male and female, travel by bicycle. I met Dr.

Bürgle, a very amiable gentleman who will see to it that I can take as many courses as I desire at the T.H. (Technische Hochschule, comparable to a technical college) or the University.

The German University has a "Schwarzes Brett" similar to our bulletin Board whereon the various departments display their notices:

T.H.
a) Thoroughness of instructor
b) Visual aids employed—charts and boardwork
c) Practical experiments performed en route
d) Order among the students
e) Greeting ("Heil" before and after)
f) Professor constantly suggests problems which are awaiting a solution

Attended a lecture in the T.H. Notice the friendliness of the people. I asked my direction of several people and all were very painstaking in giving me the correct direction. Finally one of the woman cleaners left her work and took me through a laboratory to the Hörsaal (lecture hall).

This auditorium is complete with all modern equipment. It is built like an amphitheater and can seat a goodly number. As I was sitting there students gradually came in 10 to 15 minutes before the lecture. At the appointed time (without benefit of bells) the students take their places, the professor dressed in civilians accompanied by a young assistant dressed in white lab coat enters. He gives the Nazi salute and all respond with a similar one. Then the students all sit down and the lecture begins without further ado.

The lecture is prepared to the smallest detail. The assistant having prepared the experimental apparatus and arranged the blackboards. On the blackboards various structural formulas are to be seen for the first class I attended was a lecture on Organic Chem (General).

The lecturer, Dr. Hans Fischer, continued at a rapid pace, for the students evidently had outlines of the lecture. He did not even stop talking when he performed tests for the various substances e.g. for pentosanes by adding *(see formula below)* which produces a blue color.

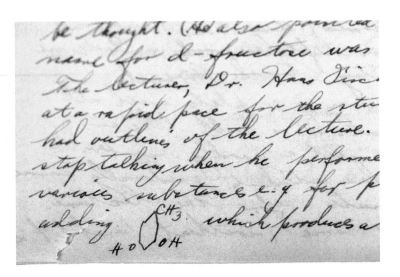

The tests are so arranged and so prepared that they all work and the Professor does not read his lecture as is so often common by us. This was a lecture in general Organic Chem(istry) but it covered more than a week's lecture of our Adv(anced) Org(anic) Chem(istry). It is noteworthy also that none of the lectures can be interrupted by questioners. The Order in the class was excellent, no laughing or talking, only strict attention. In the course of the lecture, the Prof(essor) kept suggesting unsolved problems an "Ansporn" (incentive) for the thoughtful student to seek their solution or at least to think over them. Then I went in search of another class but by the time I found the correct room it was already too late. Consequently I wandered aimlessly about the streets of Munich.

At the time, German scientists and the German educational system were often considered superior and the diary supports that belief. Discipline and obedience were in evidence. In 1938, chemists working in Berlin split the uranium atom, which led to the development of the atomic bomb. This prompted Albert Einstein to write President Roosevelt and he initiated the beginnings of what became the Manhattan Project.[25]

FROM THE DIARY—Another colorful sight met my eyes, a beer wagon from the Löwenbräu. It seemed to be a half of a wagon for one side was straight and the other slant. The horses had a gaily colored headpiece while the driver was the chief point of interest. Black pants with black boots, a bluish purple vest with a black hat and a white feather. A white shirt and a white feather on his hat. This is only one of the many picturesque figures in this city.

Then I went into Ludwigskirche. All the churches seem to be large and this one was no exception. It was built 1829-1845 by Friedrich Gärtner in Byzantine Roman style, as a room for the giant fresco by Peter Cornelius.

That evening my aunt told me of her experiences after the war (WWI) of the inflation when money (paper) became so plentiful that the workers had to carry their wages home in knapsacks and finally in 1923 when the Rentenmark was established and all the paper money became practically worthless. One Trillion paper marks equaled one Rentenmark. The people were dumbfounded. All the money they had saved and all their work was in vain. If we could realize this we could realize the need for a change in government, my aunt told me.

1939—EXPERIENCING NATIONAL SOCIALISM

July 1, 1939—Cornelius Vanderbilt Jr., Liberty magazine's roving correspondent, returned to Paris from Rome yesterday after a month's flying survey of Poland, Germany, Czecho-Slovakia, Hungary and other European trouble zones. "I'll bet my shirt there'll be no war," said Mr. Vanderbilt, on his arrival last night at the Hotel Crillon. "Germany hasn't enough wheat, oil, steel and other raw materials to wage a war successfully." [26]

FROM THE DIARY—Went to the police station this morning, Saturday July 1st to announce our arrival in Germany. Whenever a person moves, leaves the country, or comes in he must announce his departure or arrival to the police by means of an Anmeldungsschein. Three papers must be filled out by each applicant, each identical on which birth, nationality, occupation, term of stay, religion, etc. must be written. Moreover, foreigners must fill out another paper of four pages on which they must announce the birth, place and date of mother, father, wife, children, of Jewish abstraction, etc.

Two photographs are also required for this paper is also information as to which sources (financial) the person in question has recourse to defray expenses while in Germany.

There are constantly recurring themes in the paper, Treaty of Versailles, Jews in America, England, etc. I quote an interesting thought provoking citation from the Süddeutsche Sonntagspost July 1, 1939.

"Was haben England und Frankreich bisher getan um zu beweisen, dass die Brutalität und Gemeinheit von Versailles nicht gerne bei einer passenden Gelegenheit wiederholen möchten? Jeden Schritt mit dem wir uns selbst daraus befreiten, haben Sie mit einer neuen Welle der antideutschen Hetze beantwortet. Dann erst haben sie sich zunächst einmal wohl oder übel damit abgefunden. Fast keine Fesseln von Versailles wurde von ihren Urhebern freiwillig gelöst."

"What have England and France done so far to prove that the brutality and cruelty of Versailles would not likely be repeated by them at the next opportunity? They answer every step we take to liberate ourselves from it, with a new wave of anti-German propaganda. Only then have they resigned themselves to it for better or for worse. Almost no shackles of Versailles were loosened voluntarily by the originators."

The Paris Peace Conference in 1919 was called to establish peace after World War I. The Treaty of Versailles outlined the compromises reached at the conference and included the intention of forming the League of Nations (a mechanism intended to prevent another world war). The Treaty of Versailles put heavy economic debts on Germany, and required that it surrender about 10% of its prewar territory and all of its overseas possessions. It limited the size of the army and navy. Germans grew to begrudge the austere conditions. [27]

FROM THE DIARY—In the same paper was an article containing letters of a Japanese soldier to his son praising love of country and glory of dying for one's country.

It just comes to mind that I forgot to describe a lecture, which I had the pleasure to attend, also at the T.H. The Professor, a Dr. Hieber, was discussing complex salts. Cobalt salts. In his lectures he brought out the relation between color and composition, exemplifying his theory with examples. Again there were numerous illustrations as also models exemplifying the isomerism etc. A luten slide was shown and during this, I noticed that the shades were lowered and raised automatically by the touch of a button. When the Professor displays a test the students scrape their feet to signify that they have seen enough of it.

While in Bremen I noticed a bookshop window replete with anti-

50

Catholic propaganda, prominent among which were the works of Ludendorff.

> *Erich Ludendorff (1865-1937) was a German general in WWI. After the war, he became an important nationalist leader and promoter of the "stab in the back legend" which was a conspiracy theory suggesting that the loss of the war was due to the betrayal by civilians with the intention of overthrowing the government.[28] According to this theory, the leaders of the Social Democratic Party (SPD) were to take the blame for Germany's defeat, while those who had participated in the war (like Ludendorff) were portrayed as having been betrayed.*
>
> *However, Germany was weak towards the end of the war. One month before the end of the war, soldiers were deserting. The German navy mutinied in November when it was ordered to attack the Royal Navy and sabotage the armistice negotiations (which took effect on November 11, 1918).[29] Kaiser Wilhelm abdicated and Germany became a republic.*

FROM THE DIARY—In Bavaria I find that Ludendorff is not held in such high esteem, most likely due to his anti-Catholic bias and they smile knowingly when they speak of him for he died in Tutzing in a Catholic hospital, attended by Catholic sisters with a crucifix over his bed.

1939—DESCRIPTIONS OF THE COUNTRYSIDE

FROM THE DIARY—Visited a local saloon—Gaststätte Osterwaldgarten. A typical old-fashioned saloon with a stove in the middle and a bowling alley and rifle range. On the wall was a huge crucifix about three feet in length. On the side walls were pictures of Hitler and a holy picture. We got a liter of beer for about 48 pfennig, about 12 cents, and very excellent beer at that.

While we were seated there two typical Bavarians came in the usual leather shorts. On their shoulders they carried long rifles. They had come to practice target shooting and drink some beer.

On the wall was an interesting saying:

"Wer pumpen will der komme morgen
Die Pumpe muss ich erst besorgen"

This is a play on words, as "to pump" can also refer to borrowing money from others.

The Wirt (barkeeper) greeted us as we came in and as we went out we received the most courteous attention even though we only had a half liter per person.

After we left here we got a splendid view of the Kleinhesseloher See and surroundings. The majestic swans gliding arrogantly upon the (water) of this charming lake with the brown feathered ducks dodging us in and out unperturbed by the awful magnificence of their companions all contributed to giving a pleasant impression of this pleasant lake.

While paging through my papers today I came upon an excellent excerpt which I had found while on shipboard. It is a quotation from Schiller.

"Ha wie die müden Abschiedsstrahlen
Das wallende Gewölk bemalen
Wie dort die Abendwolken sich
Im Schoss der Silberwellen baden" —Schiller

The words in this stanza of a poem speak to the rays of the sun saying goodnight at sunset in the lap of the silver waves, a poetic description of the sea and the sky.

FROM THE DIARY—It reminds me exactly of the scenery that can be viewed from the ship. Every day the sky and sea combined to present a different picture though there were some who became tired of seeing nothing but sea and sky.

At sea the ocean was as blue as ink while the sky faded into a deep blue and when the moon arose its reflection cast a silver streak upon the black background. While in the North the northlight helped in forming a rosy tint above the horizon of the sea. The furrow left by the steamer was as wide as a city street and could be seen as far as the ocean was visible. When the sea was calm, as it usually was, it reminded one of a small stream flowing through desert land.

At Southampton the water was a light green, gradually fading into the light blue of the sky on the horizon. This together with the hazy atmosphere gave a picture that will long be remembered.

1939—THE IMPORTANCE OF
KEEPING COUNTRY SECRETS

FROM THE DIARY—Went to Church at St. Sylvester's. Hats not required for women. Sermon not delivered in every mass, just in one or two and these are announced previously. In the morning I went to the Deutsches Museum. This is similar to the Franklin Institute in Philadelphia with its technical and scientific exhibits.

In the hall of fame there, I noticed the bust of a Jesuit, Athanaesius Kircher S.J.[30] donated by Georgetown University. In this hall were paintings and sculptures of all the leading German scientists.

In one compartment was a collection of time pieces from oil and sand clocks up to the most complicated spring clocks. They had several clocks which told star and sun time, the day, month and year, season, etc.

. . .

For 25 pfg (cents) one can climb to the top of the tower and back. From the tower one has an unobstructed view of Munich. One can see the various church spires peering over the other houses and far in the distance can be seen the ranges of the Bavarian Alps. This evening we visited the movies and saw "The Gouverneur."[31]

Going to the movies in Germany differs quite a bit from America. There are only two aisles, one on either side. You enter on the left and take the seat furthest right that is vacant. When someone leaves he goes out by the door on the right and all others in that row now moved one seat to the right. In this theater there were four price ranges from 70 pfg (cents) to over one Mark. The 70 pfg (cents) was the furthest front, then 90 pfg (cents) etc.

The picture was well played and directed. It had several plots and counterplots prominent among which was the conflict between love for a woman and love for the (army)regiment.

Then there followed a short illustrating an excerpt from Hitler's "Mein Kampf" namely that the people should not discuss military secrets openly. Herein was shown how easily an ammunition plant might be blown up if a spy could determine its location by conversing with Germans.

Then there followed a news film. Herein was shown an American strike and how National Guards protected the strike breakers, then they showed a scene of Bavarian workers peacefully mowing hay on a hillside, then a parade being viewed by Franco in Spain, and finally the Führer inspecting a new plant for DKF automobiles.

1939—CONTINUING TO LEARN

This morning went to University and heard opening speech by the Rector. In the corridor I noticed an immense picture of Athanaesius Kircher S.J. The Rector bade us welcome and invited us to study German language and culture. Then I heard a lecture by V. Müller on History. When he entered we all remained seated and knocked on the benches and scraped our feet just as we did when the lecture was over.

German classes are scheduled on the hour e.g., 9—10 but begin 15 minutes later by virtue of what is known as "das Akademische Viertel" *(the academic quarter).* On the way home I saw a priest with a long black frock riding a bicycle, an unaccustomed sight for me.

Tuesday morning I visited a class on the Theory of Analytical Functions by Prof. Perron but it was fairly unintelligible. The next class is Obercurs I. By the way, I noticed that in the University the German students stamp their feet in approval of their professor and do not give the Nazi salute as in the T.H.

Oskar Perron, a famous mathematician, taught at the University of Munich from 1922 to 1951 and was a staunch anti-Nazi.

In 1928, Salomon Bochner, a mathematician whose career in Munich was suffering due to anti-Semitism, sought a position at Harvard. Though his bid failed, Oskar Perron tried to help him and wrote a letter to another top mathematician Carathéodory stating "The only real thing which could still help would be an invitation to Bochner from America. Thus we would have the means at hand to show the ministry even more clearly that Bochner really is somebody, and that it is embarrassing in the scientific world to make life difficult for him here." [32]

Bochner eventually left Germany in 1933 after receiving an invitation to join the faculty at Princeton University in New Jersey. He taught at Princeton until 1969, having supervised 35 doctoral dissertations. [33]

1939—THE DAILY LIFE OF A STUDENT, NAZI PARADING

FROM THE DIARY—Then followed a class by Vossler in Literature in which Dr. Vossler gave a very interesting lecture. He was very well received, the ovation lasting for several minutes. His lecture was filled with many witticisms. Very noticeable was his eulogy, rather laudatory remarks in reference to the Catholic Church's influence on Goethe.

*

Karl Vossler was forced to retire from the University of Munich in 1937, though he taught subsequent courses. He was described as a passionate German patriot, but anti-Nazi. He believed in intellectual freedom. Vossler was one of the scholars who interceded on behalf of Werner Krauss in 1943, who had been sentenced to death for his association with the Schulze-Boysen-Harnack resistance group.[34]

The Schulze-Boysen-Harnack group was engaged primarily in anti-Nazi propaganda and in helping those persecuted by the regime. The group was exposed in 1942 and more than 50 members were executed.[35]

The next class was also interesting, the History Class conducted by V. Mueller. One point that he stressed was that ever since ancient times the German body politic has been striving towards a Führer which was realized under the present system.

That afternoon we visited the Residenz Museum, the former residence of the Bavarian kings. En route to the Museum we had to pass the Feldherrn Halle where the 1st unsuccessful Nazi Putsch was held and many Nazis were killed. There is a perpetual watch here (die ewige Wache) and every German who passes the spot (on the Residenz Strasse) makes the Nazi salute. I just happened to pass as they were changing the guard. Two S.S. men bearing guns led by an officer marched in goose-step across the street and took the place of the former two guards; a very solemn ceremonial.

Dr. Thomas was our guide through the Residenz and a very fitting one because he could explain even the finest detail. The Residenz is peculiar because it is not the product of one age but an accumulation of many. Various kings added different structures. In here are to be seen Rococo, Baroque, and Louis XVI one after the other, each of which was fittingly described by our tour guide.

After our tour which lasted approximately 2 ½ hours we had coffee in the café on the veranda of the Haus der Deutschen Kunst. In Germany if you ask for coffee you receive a "Portion" which contains 2-3 cups of coffee whereas if you desire one cup you must specify the same. That evening we had a dance in the "Cherubim" Saal of the "Hotel der Vier Jahreszeiten" *(The Four Seasons)*. Here we spent a delightful evening.

Of course we had the usual introductory speeches. But then we had a violin recital by a "Herma Studeny" which was really wonderful. The soloist was apparently quite temperamental for she stood on the stage with the violin at her side until all the waiters had left the room and ceased scurrying about. The tones produced, however, were really worth hearing. She played Beethoven Romanze in G Dur and Brahms, Nachgelassener Sonatensatz in C moll both of which were well received. Then a young lady, Helga Thorn by name, sang several old folk songs, accompanying herself on the lute. Loblied auf die Musik; Hansel dein Gretelein; Wenn ich ein Vöglein wär; Spinn, spinn.

Then followed three dances by a Dolly Würzbach: Spanischer Walzer, Neapolitanisch, Bayrischer Ländler.

Then we had a dance—mostly American songs (Bye bye blues, etc). I danced with several Slovakians from whom I learned that the Slovaks like Hitler. I asked them if they had autonomy; they replied no, that they had absolute freedom. Hlinka was very well liked by them, a national hero. In former Czechoslovakia the Czechs held all the important positions and the Slovaks were relegated to subordinate roles. Furthermore, the Slovaks could understand the Czechs but not vice versa and consequently the Slovaks had to learn Czech. The true Slovaks, they claim want their freedom, only certain people in Slovakia, not real Slovaks, rather other races, did not want a free Slovakia. They laughed when I told them I thought they were suppressed (sic) by Hitler.

*

Andrej Hlinka (1864-1938), was a Slovak Roman Catholic Priest and patriot who was the leader of the Slovak autonomist opposition to the Czechoslovak government in the 1920s and '30s. Hlinka was a true Slovak patriot, but failed to see how his hostility to the Czechs was exploited by the Germans and Magyars who aimed to destroy Czechoslovakia and felt little benevolence for the Slovak cause.[36]

FROM THE DIARY—The headwaiter's brother is proprietor of the Little Old Heidelberg, Lutz, he also knows a Hoffmann Proprietor of a Ratskeller in Philadelphia. His son was serving in the English army.

This morning, Wednesday I got a hair-cut for 60 pfg (cents). 10% off for being a student. In the Student's Handbook the prices are as follows

60 pfg (cents)—II Class Shop
50 pfg (cents)—III Class Shop

I evidently had a II Class Shop. The master barber cut my hair but he had two apprentices working on two other customers. One apprentice was about 14 years old.

1939—EXPERIENCES, PERCEPTIONS, BEER

FROM THE DIARY—Went to the sport field of the Bayerische Gemeinde Bank. This is practically a country-club built by the bank for its employees. It has a swimming pool, tennis courts, track etc. As I arrived about 50 employees were engaged in mass exercises. Then they all participated in some sport, young and old. The Germans have developed a universal interest for sport and as a result they all look healthy.

We sat on the veranda and had 1 ½ liters of beer, 48 pfg (cents) for one liter, about 12 cents. Here on the veranda sat various employees taking life easy. Everyone had at least a ½ liter before him and everyone was congenial and happy. In the corner two fellows were playing chess and in the club room someone was playing records which were transmitted to us by virtue of a loud speaker. The bank bought 200 of the best records for its employees.

Greetings are very frequent in Bavaria. I had to shake hands with all the friends of my cousin on meeting and then again when leaving. I remember once I came into the house without saying "Grüss Gott" and I received the devil from my uncle.

This morning Tuesday July 6th I visited an entertaining lecture by Bürgle. He explained why some nouns have der, others die, and still others das. "Der" signifies strength and power and is associated with masculine connections. "Die" signifies weakness, fruitfulness, and is associated with feminine. Z. B Sturm (storm), Donner (thunder), Blitz (lightening), Mut (courage)—masculine, Blüte (blooms), Schürze (apron), Demut (humility)—Feminine.

But then why is lake—See preceded by "der" and See—sea by "die"? The answer is that the Germans became acquainted with the sea via the Romans. Since they were in southern Germany they were not acquainted with it personally and here it was something unknown to them, hence das Meer. Then they named a closed body of water, der See because they were acquainted with such mighty bodies of water as the Bodensee, etc. Die See came from the North where the North and Baltic Sea furnished the life giving water to the fields and consequently determined as feminine.

But how about Sonne (sun) and Mond (moon)? Well when the old German peasant saw the full moon he associated it with cold and consequently frost. Der Frost, a mighty force which might lay waste in his field. Consequently der Mond and the weaker planet, die Sonne. But in the south, in Italy and France, the sun is much more powerful and hence it is designated as masculine.

Buttmann gave a talk on the History of the Third Reich. He mentioned that at one time there were 26 parties in the Reichstag, all of which hopelessly and futilely struggled for supremacy. He also mentioned that Germany signed the Treaty of Versailles with the understanding that the other nations would also disarm. All other governments after the Treaty of Versailles were not justified because they admitted the right of foreign states to determine the form and matter of the German body politic. This the Third Reich rejected.

Research on the name Buttmann and Munich yielded only one name: Rudolf Buttmann. He was a lawyer, librarian and a staunch Nazi active in the National Socialist party. While it is not certain that he was the person who gave the lecture to the summer course in Munich in 1939, it is possible. Buttmann held the position of the Director General of the Bavarian State Library from 1935 to 1945. He was active in the Institute for the History of the New Germany and belonged to a group focused on researching the "Jewish question."

FROM THE DIARY—He mentioned his experience with Jews—how they wandered in after the War—the Galicians and how they were Communistic—set up a Communist government in Munich mostly consisting of Jews.

He also accuses the Jews of shirking military duty, of how they connived to obtain easy positions behind the lines instead of in the trenches. He said he knew one Jew who, although he had never handled horses before, obtained a position as a stable-boy to the Major, finally getting into the Quartermaster Dept. Then we had an interesting lecture by Schürer in which he contrasted the architecture of Augsburg and Nürnberg—Schwäbisch and Fränkisch.

Part 2: Settling In

1939—SOCIALIZING, LITERATURE

This afternoon we visited the Rathaus where we were officially welcomed by the Oberbürgermeister. He gave us each a book on München. Then we climbed the winding stairs to the tower from which we had a wonderful view over the entire city—to the Alps.

I noticed that practically everyone carries a schoolbag in Munich. Herein they have lunch, books, or use them to carry home goods from the store.

Our radio only reaches Munich. For this my aunt must pay two Marks per month tax. In the winter she has to give two pounds of vegetables or food for the poor and every week there is a collection to which all must contribute according to their means. Then they have to pay for Luftschutz, Arbeitsfront, etc. etc., quite a number of outlays. They also have to pay to have their chimney swept every six weeks even when it is not in use. If she has an argument with the chimney sweep he can turn around and have her chimney condemned which costs more.

This evening I attended the Ausländer Ball im Seehaus am Kleinhesselohen See. Both Ballrooms packed—many more Natives than Ausländer. Danced with a couple Danes and several native German girls. American music.

July, 1939—The last remaining Jewish shops are closed by the Nazis.[37]

FROM THE DIARY—Friday July 7th, had interesting class at the University. Hederer discussed modern German authors with us. Thomas Mann—good style, left Germany of his own accord for political reasons though Germany invited him to remain. He is said to have said on the radio in Zürich that there was no good German poet left in Germany.

Erich Maria Remarque although only 14 days in the war describes the war as folly, as something abominable whereas the Nazi authors e.g. E. Junger describes the heroic deeds and fatherland's love displayed therein.

Oscar Maria Graf, whom I heard in Philadelphia, a genial Bavarian was banned because of his Communistic tendencies or rather his description of the Revolution in "Wir sind gefangen." Furthermore Hederer jokingly remarked that he could only write Bavarian anyway.

Emil Ludwig he pictured as a fellow who wrote for a living and who having exhausted the number of men for his biographies filled with his own personal interpretation, has begun to describe the histories of rivers e.g. The Nile.

As I sat in one of the classes I noticed the following parody carved in the desk at which I was sitting. It was a parody of Goethe's well-known poem "Über allen Gipfeln ist Ruh"[38]

SOMMERSEMESTER

Über allen Bänken ist Ruh
Vom Katheder spürest du
Kaum einen Hauch
Wir träumen vom Schweigen im Walde
Warte, nur Professor, balde
Schweigest du auch

SUMMER SEMESTER

Above all the benches, it is quiet
From the lectern you feel scarcely a breath
We dream of the silence in the forest
Wait, Professor, soon you will be silent too.

1939—TRAVELING, SINGING

FROM THE DIARY—Sunday we all went to Bad Tölz by train. We rode in one of those compartment trains, eight in each compartment and inasmuch as there was no corridor through there was a toilet for each compartment right in the compartment. There were the two Danish girls, Hedin from Schweden and Mr. Alleman, Swiss student at Munich and we four Americans, Balch, Bergmann, Fr. Brown,[39] and myself.

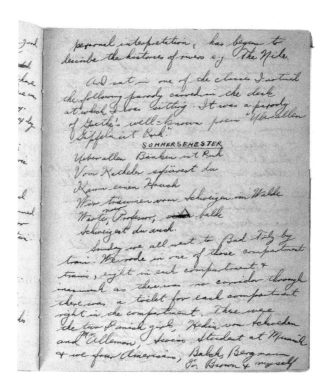

We sang plenty of songs all the way to Tölz. En route we saw a colorful scene, a parade in one of the little towns. In the van were the men all dressed up in their leather shorts all playing an instrument. Then came the women, some with Red Dirndl and a second group, all with Blue Dirndl, and of course black bodices with white aprons, a colorful sight.

1939 MUNICH, A COLORFUL CITY

FROM THE DIARY—Munich itself is a colorful sight on Sundays, everybody is dressed in his best and most colorful (clothes) even the old people.

At Tölz we alighted and walked through the town to the Isar. A very colorful town, all the quaint houses are painted with Holy pictures and on one house above each window was one of Christ's last words on the cross. Some houses had statues of the Saints and several had crucifixes in front. In the centre of the street was a fountain with a Madonna and child on top of it. As we walked down the street, Church was just leaving out, families could be seen walking in groups down the street, the men in shorts and the women in gaily colored Dirndl clothes. Even the children were dressed in shorts and Dirndl for the occasion. At the bottom of the street lay the Isar, green while on the other bank could be seen the rolling range of mountains. Before we reached the Isar we stopped in a Church—typical Baroque but so ornate and so rich that it appeared like a Church in some big city.

Then we reached the Isar. Just as we came there a raft came floating down the river. On it was a small Blasorchester (brass ensemble) and the people were dancing and singing, some of them were waving beer seidels at us—another colorful scene.

We walked back to our raft. All around us was mountainside and before us lay the swift, flowing Isar. We boarded the raft and soon we were off. We had an accordion player and we too started dancing. The raft can hold 60 with ease and in the centre, smooth boards had been placed to permit dancing with bare feet. We had two barrels of beer and the raft was furnished with huge liter steins so you can see we had an enjoyable time. In spots the Isar is very shallow and many times we had to get out and push. Most of us wore trunks and swam after the raft. Several times we rode over rapids and we passed many kayaks en route. On one place on the bank were two women, one elderly around 70 the other younger. When we came along they jodeled a song for us in harmony to which we naturally applauded. Everything was so gemütlich (comfortable, peaceful feeling) we all had a good time. We arrived at Thalkirchen at 7 o'clock. I should mention our drivers. Three Bavarians, two in front, one in the rear guiding the huge carved paddles. All dressed in shorts, all over 45. The one in front had a long pipe in his mouth the entire trip. The scenery en route was wonderful—green Isar, blue sky, green rolling mountainside.

In school we heard three lectures by Dr. Schürer on the History of Art, on the way in which Baroque was modeled by the Franks in Nürnberg and the Swabians in Augsburg. All the pictures, it was noteworthy, were pictures of churches.

Tuesday I bought several anti-Catholic books in the lobby of the University. These books were being sold along with others on Jewry and National Socialistic Philosophy on account of the fact that all the Bavarian schoolteachers had a convention here.

We had a lecture about education. Dr. Kroh explained to the class why the government was against religious education. He differentiated between functional and intentional education. The last is the typical education but the functional education deals with the situation in which people work together.

Oswald Kroh was an educator and psychologist who was very active in promoting the Nazi agenda.[40] He joined the National Socialist party in 1933 and by 1935 was named "Liaison for the German Society for Psychology to the Delegate of the Führer for the Entire Intellectual and World-View Education of the NSADP" (Nationalsozialistische Deutsche Arbeiterpartei, the Nazi Party).

In 1942 Kroh was recommended by the local head of the Nazi Professors' League and advanced to the Head of the Berlin Psychological Institute, a highly prestigious placement. He was dismissed from his position in December 1945 and struggled to rehabilitate himself after the fall of the Nazi party.

"Consider the following," said Prof. Kroh. "Of what use is religious education if someone with such an education would come into a world which is atheistic? That means that the functional and intentional ideas are at odds. However, this is the Nazi education; it is much better that the Nazis try to order life, and thus to organize the schools, that they both work to a single goal, that is to an independent Germany."

1939—MUSIC, MEETING NEW PEOPLE

FROM THE DIARY—On Tuesday I went to Alfred's. There I played zither with Maria and she also sang along. On Wednesday we went to Lake Starnberg. We left the train station at 7.45 and were there in a half an hour. On the way I talked to a German student about the T.H. He was in Czechoslovakia last year with the Panzer tanks. On Monday he has to report to East Prussia to help with the harvest. All students have to help with the harvest as there are not enough workers and due to the political tension, the Poles are not helping the way they did in the past.

He described the foreign occupation of the Rhine because he came from Düsseldorf on the Rhine. The occupation lasted 10 years. The French were less popular than the English because of their rudeness. There were also separatists that wanted the Rhine to separate from Germany, and therefore were friendly to the French. Locals didn't want to operate the railways because many of the bridges were blown up and consequently foreigners were called in. Communism became stronger and then the National Socialist (N.S.) government came to power and was successful in this area.

The Rhineland was a natural barrier between France and Germany and was a "demilitarized zone" after WWI. In 1935, when the Saar region voted to reunite with Germany, it was technically a violation of the Treaty of Versailles, but when other countries did not object, the tacit approval provided Hitler with the opportunity to test the boundaries of the Treaty even further. In fact, in 1936 he marched German troops into the Rhineland, which was a direct violation of the Treaty agreed upon at the end of WWI.

We traveled to Starnberg Lake in a steamer, providing a wonderful view. We saw the place where Ludwig II died, he threw himself in the water, and where he is buried. Then 1 ¼ hours later we arrived in Seeshaupt.

Here I traveled in a canoe with Hohefeld. Then we had a nice meal. There I talked to a Hungarian. He described the circumstances in Hungary. Jews, he said, make up a large part of the aristocracy. They control the press and are therefore hated. They seek the help of the Catholic Church even though they are not treated the way they are in Germany. Imredi *(Imrédy)* put the anti-Semitic laws in force and they made a lot of noise that one of his great grand-parents was Jewish. Relatively speaking, there are many more Jews in Hungary than there ever were in Germany.

Béla Imrédy was a right wing politician and the Prime Minister of Hungary from 1938-9. He was born Catholic and considered pro-German and pro-Italian, which angered the moderate politicians in the country. He resigned from office when his Jewish ancestry was revealed but continued to serve in leadership positions. His close collaboration with the Nazis led to his execution as a war criminal in 1946.[41]

After this meal, we went about another hour by foot to Lauterbach Mühle on the Ostersee. Lively Place. Different islands in the lake. Alps in the background. Swam about 300-400 meters to an island and back. Viewed the inside of the Inn "Zur Lauterbach Mühle." On the wall of one of the rooms there is the poem "To Lauterbach etc." printed in big letters and in the corner stands a large crucifix. We sat on the veranda and drank a glass of beer—we had a beautiful view of the lake—cows grazing on a hillside above us. Then we walked back to Seeshaupt where we took the train back to Munich.

The German forest is stately. All the spruces stand at attention just as if they were street posts, lofty towers.

1939—CATHOLICISM AND NATIONAL SOCIALISM
CANNOT BE RECONCILED

Though it is not certain if it is the same person, Rudolf Buttmann served as Assistant Secretary of State and Head of the Cultural Policy from 1933-1935. He participated in the 1933 negotiation with the Holy See "Reichskonkordat." The treaty was to guarantee the rights of the Roman Catholic Church in Germany, and require clergy to abstain from working on or behalf of any political parties. The Nazis aimed to eliminate the Church's influence by restricting its activities.

FROM THE DIARY—On Thursday, I heard Buttmann again. He stressed that Catholicism and National Socialism still stand in opposition.

In the evening I heard Hans Brandenburg, the poet. He read some of his poems in the little Hall of the University. He read "Father Öllendorf" and "Pankratz the Shepherd Boy." I didn't like the first one as it went into too much detail. It described how four children were playing and fighting before going to bed and for this description he used at least 3 pages, which is very uninteresting and boring. Afterwards we talked at the Bavarian Riding School, a beer garden. There we spoke with Hans Brandenburg and Vesper, another poet. I also talked to a PhD in Chemistry. He will ask if I can get a job in Germany. He also wants to see America, but the chemists all with compulsory military service, are forbidden to go abroad for a longer period of time.

All night they prepared for the Day of German Art. They tested the loudspeakers, the lights, etc. For months they had already erected posts in the streets, flags were hung, wreaths were hung that were more than 8 feet in diameter.

1939—CASUALTIES OF WAR

FROM THE DIARY—Today on Tuesday I learned that I can still join a summer course at any university. I will also get free room and board. I first have to think about it. I also received 3 tickets for the theater, each costing 1.30 Marks. Goethe's Faust, Kleist's Amphitryon and Iphigenia in Tauris.

Friday afternoon we took a tour of the Austria-Cigarette Factory. The factory looked more like an apartment building than a factory. It was quite clean and in each hallway there were sayings from the "Führer" hanging in frames on the wall. After the tour I walked home with a Spaniard. She was studying Arabic and Latin in Germany. Ancient Arabic is considered a classical language in Spain. I asked her if she eventually wanted to teach. She answered that she preferred to help a professor in research since many ancient texts were lost during the Civil War in Spain.

She was in Madrid when the war broke out. Even before the war, she said, the communists were in power because if one wasn't a communist, it was impossible to get help from the Government (like in the US). When the war broke out, most people thought it would only last 3-4 days. Corpses lay in the streets many times for 3-4 days. A bomb blasted once, 4 meters from her and killed 5 people. At night you could hear how the communists shot down the nationalists and those friendly towards them, taking them to a wall and shooting. This screaming drove many people crazy as the shooting of the non-combatants continued. Her Father was sheltered by the English Ambassador and she fled to France.

When the conservatives in Spain failed in their attempt to overthrow the government, a civil war broke out (Spanish Civil War 1936-1939). The Nationalist rebels were supported by Fascist Italy and Nazi Germany. The Republicans were supported by the Soviet Union and volunteers from Europe and the United States. Republican violence took place early in the war before law was reestablished, but the Nationalist violence was part of a deliberate policy of terror.[42]

The Basques, she explained to me, speak a language that is similar to Sanskrit. It has nothing in common with Spanish. The Basques are a little dumb, very religious and very sensitive. Had they known that they would be fighting with the communists, she said they would have never fought against the nationalists. When I asked her if the Church was guilty for the war occurring, she said to me "we are all guilty."

1939—THE THEATER AND HITLER

FROM THE DIARY—Tonight I saw Goethe's "Faust" in the "Prinzregententheater." It lasted from 7 until 12 midnight and it was wonderful. The staging was incredible—the witch's kitchen, how the stage turned as Mephisto led Faust over the mountains—no effort or money was spared in creating this charming image. Gretchen was portrayed as particularly pitiful. It tugged at the heartstrings. In the midst of the drama Mephisto complained that Gretchen's mother gave the jewelry box to the priest because it didn't belong to her and he commented that "Only the Church can digest injustice" which resulted in thunderous applause from the spectators in the front rows, apparently anti-clericals.

August 15, 1939, ROME—The works of famous writers, including many Jews, and such books as the Nick Carter series of red-blooded adventures that thrilled American boys a generation or two ago, as well as Emil Ludwig's biography of Lincoln, have been condemned officially as unsuited to the Fascist spirit. Booksellers and librarians received the list, which included books that have been seized and destroyed and others of which the sale has been forbidden. The condemned authors include Casanova, Balzac, Boccaccio, Machiavelli, Rabelais, Voltaire and Poe.[43]

FROM THE DIARY—Today, Saturday the 15th I noticed that every morning when I walk by a construction site the workers are drinking a half liter of beer, a Munich tradition. I went to the train station to meet the Witzelhofers. It looked like New York. The sight was incredible. People flocked from all over to attend the Day of German Art in Munich. Saturday night I saw "Amphitryon" by Kleist at the Residenz

Theater. The theater is quite small and was made only for the nobility. There are private boxes all around the sides where I had my seat. The play "Amphitryon" is about the loyalty of Alcmene, wife of Amphitryon.

When the Play was finished we went outside and noticed a throng of people in front of the State Theater next door. Inside "Tannhäuser" was being performed and Hitler was in the audience.

The people started to call "We want to see our Führer." Then the windows of the 2nd floor of the Opera house opened and Hitler greeted the people from the window. I could see him very well as I had my opera glasses with me.

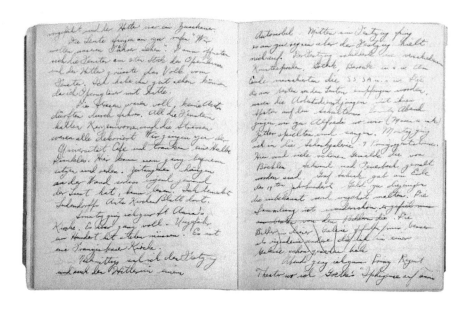

The streets were full; no cars were allowed to drive through. All the windows had candles and the streets were all decorated. We went to the University Café and drank a half liter dark beer. Here one can sit and talk comfortably. Newspapers hang on the wall so that anyone with an interest can read. I noticed Ludendorff's Anti-Church paper there.

1939—CATHOLIC MASS, HITLER IN A PARADE

Sunday I went to St. Anna's Church. It was completely full. About a hundred people had to stand. It's a Franciscan Church.

In the afternoon I saw the parade and also Hitler in an automobile. In the middle of the parade it began to rain, but the parade continued. The parade depicted the various artistic periods, Gothic, Baroque, etc. At the end marched the S.S. and the S.A. etc. Those that were best received by the people were the labor service youth with their spades on their shoulders.

Sunday night we went to Alfred's where we (Maria and I) played zither and sang. Monday I went to the Schack-Galerie - 9 Prinzregenten Street. Here there are many beautiful paintings that have been painted by Böcklin, Schwind, and Feuerbach. Towards the end of the 19th century Count Schack gave money to the unknown and unhonored painters. The collection is beautiful.

In the evening I went to the Prinzregententheater where I saw Goethe's "Iphigenia in Tauris." It was very well played. Iphigenia has become a priestess. She heard that her Father Agamemnon is dead and that her mother Clytaemnestra killed her father when he came back from the Trojan War. And that her mother Clytaemnestra was killed in revenge by her brother Orestes. Orestes comes to her and has gone insane but her faith in him and love for him cures his madness.

Today I bought lederhosen. A Californian told me that the American

Consul asked him if he could be ready to leave the country with 12 hours preparation time.

FROM A YELLOW PAD OF PAPER—In August we began reading reports in the newspaper that Germans were being killed in the Polish Corridor which separated East Prussia from Germany. The rhetorical question kept appearing regularly, "How long can we tolerate this?" The answer came on September 1, 1939 when Germany invaded Poland. We had planned to return to Philadelphia in the middle of September. Now that was no longer possible. German ships no longer sailed the Atlantic. The country was at war.

1939—HOUSE SEARCHES IN MUNICH, GERMAN OPPRESSION

FROM THE DIARY—Many house searches conducted. Once Pepi wanted to go out of the house during a search and there was a soldier on the other side already taking aim at him. Aunt Loni once went around the corner and the shooting followed her. A lot of shooting and stealing. Jews sent their money to Luxembourg, America, etc., resulting in inflation.

Eisner, a Jew (said to be from Poland) came from Berlin and became President.

Kurt Eisner was a German-Jewish journalist, theater critic and pacifist. As a socialist journalist and statesman, he organized the Socialist Revolution, and in November 1918, he overthrew the Wittelsbach monarchy in Bavaria, created the Bavarian Republic, and demanded peace. He became the first Prime Minister. He introduced the eight-hour workday and female suffrage, but his party suffered heavy losses in Bavarian elections in January 1919. He was murdered the day he intended to resign in February 1919 by a nationalist and anti-Semitic university student, Count Anton von Arco auf Valley. The assassination radicalized the political climate in Munich.[44]

On Wednesday we took a trip to Tegernsee and Schliersee. We left around 8.30 from the Holzkirchner train station. We arrived at Tegernsee approximately 10 o'clock. The views are magnificent. The lake is completely encircled by mountains. They are named the Gindelalm. We went by foot to Neureuth. The road was all up hill. It took about an hour. At the top there was a beautiful restaurant with a magnificent view of the Tegernsee and the Alps. After we stayed here for a time, two Bavarians came by and played zither and guitar. I also played the zither accompanied by the guitar. My student friends were astonished when I played. Then we went down the mountain to Schliersee. It took about 2 hours. Schliersee is also beautiful, everywhere the high mountains encircled us. There we swam and from there we went back home. On the way home we saw many crosses by the roadside.

On the train I spoke with a Dane. He explained a few things to me about his homeland that I didn't know.

Before 1864 Eckernförde belonged to Denmark. In 1864 Germany took everything up to the town of Esbjerg. 1920—after a plebiscite all the Danes up to the current border went back to Denmark.

Under German rule, Danish was banned in schools. But the Germans in current Denmark have German schools, German teachers and senior teachers. The Danes still in Germany have Danish schools but lose a lot of help or benefits when they send their children to these schools. Frequently, word came from Berlin that they don't have to send their children to the Hitler Youth, but in spite of that it's required by the local officials.

The German response to the oppression of the Danes is that the German Commissioner for Education was guilty but that he hoped that through these measures he would win approval from the government.

1939—RUMORS, MUSIC AND BEER

FROM THE DIARY—Thursday we went to the airport (Munich) where we made a roundtrip sightseeing flight. We flew as far as the Ludwigs

Church, partially over the English Garden and back. Sunday we went to Augsburg. Here we went to Mass in the church of St. Ulrich - a very large church. Here we also found out that a neighbor of Pepi is returning from the East Front after 3 months.

But on Sunday I heard from Fritz that various soldiers had been vaccinated again and that there were German soldiers in Romania. We went through the Swabian city of Augsburg with Pepi.

Made a bicycle trip to the Jugoslvian border to the Platsch. Stopped in about 8 inns where we had ½ liter wine, next time beer, etc. Photographed customs inspector at the border. Got caught in the rain and stayed in an inn for about 1 ½ hours and then took the train at Ehrenhausen to Leibnitz. Everybody greets everybody else in the inns and on the way. Saw many women and girls carrying pails of water on their head since there has been a drought in this area. Most of the women and girls go barefoot. Many oxen teams to be seen. The road we took was a former Roman road and the stones are yet to be seen. Viewed the colossal monuments in front of the mausoleum of the bishop of Ehrenhausen. He was a Jew, Kohn from Olmütz.

Leibnitz is a city in the Austrian state of Styria and the birthplace of George's mother. It's a small town with less than 10,000 residents and is south of Graz.

August 16 visited Schloss Seggau Keller. Saw huge barrels, many with the insignia of a bishop on them. Took 3 pictures with flash powders down below and then had a liter of Luttendorf with my cousin Florian. This was the best wine I tasted so far in Steiermark. It is grown in the winefields of Jugoslavia which belong to the bishop. The Schloss, Keller, Wine fields, etc. belong to the bishop for Nutzniessung (usufruct—meaning having the legal right to income from the estate though not owning the estate) only he cannot give them away as inheritance to his relatives. The Gut (estate) goes to the next bishop. The Kellermeister must know the Kiefertrade i.e.,

Barrels, he also must know wine and wine chemistry. For salary he gets 80 marks per month with full board for himself and his wife.

Left Leibnitz for Graz. Visited the Schlossberg with its beautiful winding paths. In the evening visited the Gaststätte zum Goldenen Ross. Here Undredl treated us as he did so often. Excellent music by a Tyroler orchestra consisting of two horns, accordion, harp and drums. The harp player was exceptionally good as was evidenced by the solos he played.

The wine is brought to the table in large funnels connected to a stand. The guests draw the wine as they want it.

Following day we visited Schlossberg again zum Goldenen Ross and the Graz Ratskeller. In the latter we heard an excellent Wiener Schrammel Trio consisting of a violin, accordion and contra guitar and two good singers. One of the singers was dressed as an Indian maharajah and sang comical ditties always ending up with the refrain "O du mein Indien, wie bist du so schön" to the tune of "O du mein Österreich." August 20, my 21st birthday I spent in the morning in Graz, then we left for Munich, a 10 hour trip with Schnellzug (express train).

August 21 saw a huge line of cars before a gasoline tank, not long later there was a sign "Leer" (empty) tagged to it.

August 23, 1939—Molotov-Ribbentrop Pact[45] signed between Germany and the Soviet Union, stated that neither country would ally or aid the enemy, nor would either country engage in aggression against the other.

August 24, 1939—As details of the Molotov-Ribbentrop Pact become public, Chamberlain (U.K.) recalls Parliament earlier than planned, resulting in a War Powers Act, positioning for potential conflict.

FROM A YELLOW PAD OF PAPER—Back in Munich, I sought means of employment. The University had received a request from a girl who wanted to be tutored in English. I immediately visited the family. However, when the door opened and I explained the purpose of my call,

I could see their jaws drop in disappointment. The mother explained that they had wanted an American. Unfortunately I showed up in Lederhosen and spoke in the local dialect. However, I was soon able to convince them of my Yankee Doodle roots by recalling some of the comic strips that were popular in our newspapers and with which the girl was familiar.

It seemed that the parents had divorced and the daughter wanted to visit her father who was working for Eastman Kodak in Rochester, NY. He had sent her American newspapers that contained comic strips.

FROM THE DIARY—....also have a student whom I am to teach English lessons. Hatty Menrad—born in Rochester NY—left when 6 years old and now cannot speak English.

In the Hofbräuhaus celebrated Abschiedsfeier (going away party) for Liliana Fratini from Arrezzo (Italy). Every day new horrible deeds are pictured in the paper. The Germans are being brutally mistreated by the Poles, the German customs officials are being shot at and the latest headline is "Poland threatens Danzig with Hungerblockade"

Just found a copy of a sign which I saw on the walls of the Gaststätte "zum Goldenen Ross" in Graz.

Der grosse Feind der Menschheit wohl (The worst enemy of man)
Ist sicherlich der Alkohol (Is certainly alcohol)
Doch in der Bibel steht geschrieben (But it's written in the Bible)
Du sollst auch deine Feinde lieben (You should also love your enemies)

1939—INCITING FEAR, PREPARATIONS, BUT TRAVEL TO ESLARN ANYWAY, UNCLE LEAVES FOR THE WAR

August 25, 1939—Letter from US Consulate in Munich telling all Americans to leave Germany at once.

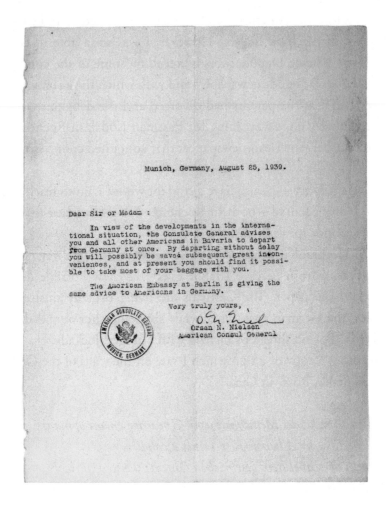

Munich, Germany, August 25, 1939.

Dear Sir or Madam :

In view of the developments in the international situation, the Consulate General advises you and all other Americans in Bavaria to depart from Germany at once. By departing without delay you will possibly be saved subsequent great inconveniences, and at present you should find it possible to take most of your baggage with you.

The American Embassy at Berlin is giving the same advice to Americans in Germany.

Very truly yours,

Orsan N. Nielsen
American Consul General

FROM THE DIARY—Friday at 10 o'clock Smoky informed me that the Consul General advised all Americans to leave Germany immediately. Some of the fellows intend to go to Switzerland. All rooms are taken in Zürich, 300 D. An American Professor (Dartmouth) told us that there are many demonstrating in England. The people shout "Down with Chamberlain" "We want Churchill." Evidently the English want to step in and fight. Yesterday the French and English left Germany. Saturday left for Eslarn.

Eslarn is the small Bavarian town where George's father came from.

As we came to the trolley car we saw a big army truck. Men in civilian clothes with small suitcases were climbing in back. Mobilization. On the other side were several army trucks with soldiers testing the equipment-telephone and wireless. Arrived at the station. Packed with people. Six ticket sellers with about 30 in each line. Train to Weiden was packed—Red Cross nurses, officers, etc. People grim—no frivolity. Arrived at Weiden. No alcoholic beverages in station restaurant. Wagner music on radio. Took Bockel train to Eslarn. Goes slower than a train. Toots horn and blows whistle and bell at every crossing because there are no gates at the crossing. Arrived at Eslarn, met relatives. Went to the Gasthaus that night. March music and Wagnerian music, no light music. Men grim, many were drafted.

Wagner was said to be a favorite composer of Adolf Hitler. The image of a country going to war, its civilians fearful in anticipation of the repercussions, all against the backdrop of a Wagnerian selection, creates a crystal clear image that is startling and disturbing at the same time. The idyllic Germany was slowly disappearing.

Nobody spoke enthusiastically all spoke cynically but resignedly. My Uncle, 43, with 5 small children, and a large farm, was drafted. Gasthaus comparatively empty.

Next morning saw same Uncle off. Everybody cried. Women, veterans who knew what war meant and the men themselves. The kids realized something was in the air and several of them cried out loud.

….Therefore we had to leave at 1.00 o'clock. Arrived in Weiden at 3 o'clock and took a Schnellzug (fast train) to Munich, packed to the doors. On the way we saw many Flak. Soldiers patrolled bridges and stations. Airport at Schleissheim had 5 military planes all set to fly. Surrounded by Flak—with shelters (camoflauged) for the soldiers. Passed several freight trains loaded with army supplies, guns, trucks, etc.

Arrived in Munich—nurses all set to leave—same uniforms as ours save for the brown instead of blue. Schwabingerbräu packed, Gasthäuser filled. School on Hausheimerstrasse being used as a barracks. Many army trucks in front of it. Listened to News on radio—The list of materials for which Bezugscheine (coupons) are required was read off. Das ist nicht eine Notmassnahme sondern eine Vorsichtsmassnahme. (This is not an emergency measure, but a precautionary measure.)

The country George had grown to love was fading and the curtain of war was drawn.

1939—BORDERS CLOSING

FROM THE DIARY—Monday 28th went to Consulate many people— all wanting to know how to get out of Germany. Consul Bauer spoke at intervals as he waited for news per telephone. One woman just arrived from Rome. The train which was supposed to go to Munich stopped at Kufstein. There the conductor shouted "Alle aussteigen" (everyone off) and after all passengers had alighted the train rolled forward. No further possibilities of train connections were present so she and several other passengers chipped in and hired a car to Munich. One woman who had been advised by the Consul to go to Holland was also there. She had been refused entry into Holland because she had no proof that she could book passage out of Holland although she had cabled her husband to send her the necessary money to Rotterdam. Still she couldn't prove that the money would arrive in Rotterdam. Holland allows a maximum of a 24 hour stay there. On the radio we heard that France has shut the borders. In the consulate I learned that Denmark had already closed the frontier. The Hansa which had left Hamburg for Southhampton was recalled. No German ships can leave port. All English ships are packed until September 20. American government is trying to persuade private steamship lines to reroute South American steamers to Germany. The American Consul heard via English news that when the planes landed in Stockholm the people ran onto the field to get a place. All airships are packed. Switzerland is full. The consul does not advise Italian ships inasmuch as if a sea battle takes place it will take place in the Mediterranean. Talked with a Philadelphian Schönberger at the Consul's. He heard via short-wave from Strasbourg France and Poland that Roosevelt had sent messages to Beck of Poland and Hitler. Nothing was in the German papers. Beck answered, Hitler did not.

Learned from a Bulgarian medical student (female) that the Bulgarian Consul told her that Bulgaria and Hungary had mobilized. Romania had mobilized 4 months previously. Bulgaria and Hungary want parts of Romania which they owned before the war. Bulgaria she said had made a pact with Germany, a month previously, and hence expects aid from the latter. She told me of many alleged brutalities committed by the Romanians. Today is the last day for purchases without cards (Bezugscheine). The stores were so crowded that they had to close in the afternoon.

August 30, 1939—Poland begins mobilization against Nazi Germany, all able-bodied men up to the age of 40 have been called for military service.[46]

August 31, 1939—Operation Himmler commences, whereby Nazi German troops impersonate Polish troops to stage a series of "false flag" operations, giving the pretext for the invasion of Poland.[47]

Bob Simmons, I heard, 2 weeks ago went to Garmisch Partenkirchen with some Germans. Passport stolen—SS man caught 2 days later. Consul cautioned us to watch our passports. Two were stolen in the last 12 hours at the railroad station. One American passport I am told is worth 3000 RM.

FROM A YELLOW PAD OF PAPER—Since Italy did not enter the war in the beginning, there was an opportunity to return to the States on an Italian ship. But this required the purchase of tickets. I immediately wrote a friend asking him to lend me the necessary funds.

FROM THE DIARY—Tuesday heard that people stood in box-cars for 10 hours in order to reach Munich from Vienna. France closed the German border. Swiss students have left. Students have dwindled to such a small number that there is only 1 Oberlehrer instead of 2 and also only one middle course. We all went to the Neue Pinakothek for a Besichtigung (visit). When we got there we were informed that all pictures were in the air raid cellar or "Luftschutzraum." This was true for all galleries and museums throughout Germany. The English and French had done this several weeks ago.

Paris school children have been taken outside the city. Every day the Poles are becoming more brutal. Today the V. Beobachter (Observer) relates a tale wherein German children were burned before the eyes of their mothers. Passed the Platzl, still room left at 8.00 o'clock, when the shows should start—something very rare.

Wednesday went to a Wirtshaus (Inn) this morning for a glass of beer and a Schweinswurst (pork sausage) at a table opposite me sat an old blind Bavarian. He had a large, flowing white beard and had a Seppl Hat on. Looking off into space he was playing folk songs, Ländler on a zither. When he finished he drank some beer and groped his way from table to table where he got his tips from the patrons. Before he was half-way around a waiter gave him a hand and guided him to the remaining tables. When he finished collecting he sat down again and played. Before I left I noticed a kindly old woman come over and give him one of her Schweinswurst which he promptly devoured.

Everyday more soldiers are leaving, on Saturday my cousin Alfred must go.

Thursday evening I noticed that in the Gasthauses the radios were crowded, everybody wanted to hear the news.

Friday morning arrived at school had a class with Hartl and then were told that the Reichstagsitzung (session of the Reichstag or Parliament) was on the Radio. We went into a huge Hörsaal (lecture room), supplied with a loudspeaker. Scrubwomen and janitors, professors, doctors and students sat, listening intently. During every pause the whole auditorium hummed with whispers. As soon as a word was spoken on the radio, every sound stopped and everyone listened as intently as before. Hitler's speech was one of the most dramatic a statesman could give. He offered himself as the first soldier for his country and named in grim order his successors.

This historic speech given by Hitler marked the exact moment on September 1st when Germany declared war on Poland. The expression "Seit 5.45 Uhr wird jetzt zurückgeschossen!" [48] *is infamous. In English it translates to "we have now been returning fire since 5.45 am" and Hitler continued, "—and from now on we will retaliate bomb for bomb."*

After the speech we had a brief lecture on Literature by Hederer. Just back from Switzerland his presentation was far below what his former lectures were. His nerves were wrecked the same as everyone else's.

During the radio transcription of the Reichstagsitzung a letter was delivered to one of the professors. He read it and left the hall. Five minutes later he returned and turning to the assembly shouted "Luftschutzraum einnehmen" (to the air raid shelters). Immediately about 5—6 women came running down the steps and made their exit.

After Hederer's class we had a brief closing exercise and the Ausländerkurse (foreign courses) were abruptly brought to a close until further notice. This closing was the result of an edict issued by the Reich.

We took several pictures, i.e., we students, and then the two Spaniards, a Hungarian girl and I planned to go rowing. We were to meet at 3.30 at St Hildegard's Pension where the Spaniards live. When I got there the sister informed me that the Spanish girl had left. They had intended to leave that day but airplane service had been stopped.

On all the trolley cars were signs "Ab heute dauernd Verdunkelung."

(From today on, continuing blackouts). I went paddling in a paddle boat alone on Kleinhesseloher See, took several pictures of the swans and then went to see Sepp Heiss. Nobody home. Returned that night but he was still working. All lights were turned off or dimmed. Trolley cars had purple lights on front and the sides. When they turned a corner they had red side arms jutting out to signify that they were about to turn. Inside the lights were covered only for a very small space. All vehicles moved slowly.

At the street corners, small lamps as used on construction jobs, were hung on wooden supports. Automobile lights were darkened, you could hardly see them. A full moon helped one see his way. The streets were not empty. They had the usual number of pedestrians. The locales were filled. All homes had huge black drapes or shades over the windows. I visited the Hofbräuhaus, Festsaal was closed but the Schwemm and Trinkstuberl were full of people. Had a liter of export dunkel (dark beer) at 52 pfg (cents). No singing but plenty of talking. In the Schwemm there is usually a tough crowd. Today there were also many soldiers. After leaving here I took a street car home. Walking from the "Platzl," the streets loomed like silhouettes out of the darkness. The rough outline of the houses as they wound about the old alleys and streets formed a pleasing impression. On the car, which was full, I heard that Germany had captured several Polish towns in the Walsa territory. On arriving home, I said goodbye to Alfred. Tante Loni, Mother, and Uncle Pepi all cried. He tried to cheer them up but they couldn't see anything cheerful in War. Went to bed early.

September 1, 1939—Germany invades Poland; WWII events have been triggered. War has begun.[49]

1939—NO WAY OUT—INADEQUATE FINANCES

FROM THE DIARY—Saturday, visited the Consul. Gloomy Gus, the Consul's secretary told me that Britain had sent an ultimatum to Germany to take her troops out of Poland. And that at 2.00pm England was going to declare War. I asked him how he could be so positive. He answered that the English Parliament was to meet at 2pm which was the moment to declare war. "Without a doubt," chanted Gloomy Gus, with such a sour puss that many an undertaker would envy with genuine professional jealousy. "Without a doubt this is going to be a world war." I am still waiting to hear news from England. Gloomy Gus is a typical student, tall, thin, spectacled, young, assured that what he says is gospel truth. He is a sadistic type who derives the keenest enjoyment from watching the anxious expressions on other people's countenances when he describes in minute details how the political situation is and how terrible it may become. The day before Frank and I asked him how we could get out of the country he said through Holland and asked us if we had any American dollars. We replied in the negative. Raising his eyebrows as if shocked by our negligence he yodeled "Cable at once for American money." At the time I was reading the "New Yorker" which was in the Consul's office and so I had no desire to leave right away. "I mean immediately" says Gloomy Gus noticing our care-free attitude "The cables might be closed at any minute!"

Poor Gus, he hates to see us come in anymore. We just can't appreciate the seriousness of the situation. But it is true that we need American Dollars to gain entry into Holland or Belgium.

Every individual needs $100 in US currency. So it is clear that Beichl & Co. will stay in Munich until the Salvation Army or someone takes up a collection.

The papers announce the mobilization of France and England.

Alfred came in his uniform today. He leaves next week for the front as a "Sanitäter" (paramedic). His shoes were soaking wet. On his belt clasp was the German Eagle, above it "Gott mit uns" (God with us) and beneath it palm branches (or olive). Went out again visited Café Perzil and HB. Came home at one. Streets have normal amount of people.

September 3, 1939—The U.K., France, New Zealand, Australia, and India (via Viceroy) declare war on Germany.[50] *Oceanliner S.S.*

Athenia becomes the first British civilian casualty of the war when it is torpedoed by a German submarine in the Atlantic Ocean.[51]

Sunday 9:00 Mass. Gospel "Can't serve two masters" thought it appropriate. Sermon lousy. Singing good. Organ music excellent. Practically whole congregation (very full) stayed for benediction.

FROM A YELLOW PAD OF PAPER—Although the country was at war, life was fairly normal. I visited the Platzl downtown, which featured the comedian Weiss Ferdl. Sing alongs were always part of the program. After singing some German songs he suggested "Let's sing a song for our Allies, the Italians" and we sang "Santa Lucia." Then he said, "Let's sing a song for our cousins across the Channel" and we sang "It's a long way to Tipperary." I think Weiss Ferdl and I were the only ones who knew that number. Note that Germany and England were at war, although no bombs had yet been dropped on either country.

Weiss Ferdl was a comedian and actor. He was also a member of the Nazi party. He was labeled a Mitläufer in the denazification proceedings. A Mitläufer is a person who was not charged with a Nazi crime, but whose involvement with the Nazi regime was considered important. Others stated that he was not a Nazi but an opponent who was monitored by the Gestapo to ensure no jokes were made against the Nazi leadership.[52]

FROM THE DIARY—Visited the Platzl. Weiss Ferdl[53] sang in different languages, Italian, Russian, after which there was much applause. Then he said, "We must not forget our dear encirclers" and sang a French song, and then "It's a Long Way to Tipperary" and after that even a Polish song. I went to the Platzl at 6 o'clock and was the first one there. At 8 the place was only half full. Before that I was in front of the Hofbräuhaus. A car came down the street and a man and a woman stepped out. They handed out a special edition of the Münchner Neuesten. The headline was "Germany rejects England's Ultimatum." The situation here is very tense. Only the United States Line and the Italian Line will accept our ship tickets. If we want to take a US ship we have to travel to Holland. We need $100-$150 in US currency before being allowed to cross the border. In Italy the ship's passage costs $160 which means we have to pay an additional $60 in currency for our ship's fare. Additionally we would need money to buy train tickets from Brenner (Brennero) to Genoa. Was in the Sterneckerbräu this week. Completely full. Baierl is a good comic. Jolly atmosphere like in the Platzl. Blackouts every night.

Sunday evening they said that Russia had mobilized and that English aircraft were forced into a battle in Belgium.

1939 AIR RAIDS AND FEAR, BEING IN THE MOMENT

FROM THE DIARY—Mittwoch (Wednesday) September 13, started work as a laborer on the renovation of a house. I had applied there the previous day, much to the surprise of the foreman. The work is hard, shoveling sand and cement for five hours or tossing old bricks and rubbish from the cellar up to the pavement, a good distance. Wednesday night rather Thursday morning at 2 o'clock I was awakened by the screaming of sirens, the Fliegeralarm (air raid). Dressing hurriedly I ran downstairs, opened the door and guided the people from neighboring houses to the Luftschutzkeller (air raid shelter). My aunt brought medicine in a basket. The sirens kept screaming for about 20 minutes, then the Entwarnungsignale (air raid cancellation siren) was sounded, a long wail which is kept at one tone.

The next day one of the laborers told me that French airplanes had dropped leaflets in the vicinity of Munich.

FROM A YELLOW PAD OF PAPER—On another occasion I was walking along Leopoldstrasse in Schwabing when I saw a sign "Arbeiter gesucht." (seeking workers) This time I was not in Lederhosen but in shirts and pants and to top it off I was wearing white shoes that were the style back home. I looked up the boss (der Polier) who looked askance at my white shoes and said, "I don't know what you have in mind, but I need workers. Show up for work tomorrow morning at 7am."

The job involved renovating an apartment house and was hard work. Fortunately, there was a "Brotzeit Pause" (coffee break, "bread" break) of five minutes at 9am when we could order a Mass Bier (1 liter) which one of the men fetched on a bricklayer's hod. We could also order beer in the afternoon but we had to drink it as we worked. I was the only American. The others were Czechs, Croats, and other foreigners. The Polier always addressed me with the polite "Sie." Once he came to me asking me to explain to the other workers what he wanted them to do, since they did not seem to comprehend. When I explained this to them, they laughed and said, "We understand him, we just don't want to do it."

FROM THE DIARY—Most of the laborers where I work come from Jugoslavia and speak little or no German. One of them who spoke good German explained that he was a Serb from the Batschka sector in the neighborhood of the Banat. He claims that there are 1 ½ million Germans in his neck of the woods and that they all want to be annexed to Germany. There is much unemployement where he lives. Every morning I go to work about 10 minutes to seven. Already there is a long line of women, approximately 20 to 30, waiting to buy meat. Meat is scarce and hence the people have to buy it early if they want any. At seven we start work. At 9 o'clock we have a 15-minute "Brotzeit." One of the fellows goes to a saloon and buys wurst and beer. We usually drink a liter of beer then and several sandwiches. From 12-1 we have dinner and at 2 o'clock we drink another liter. This is no official "Brotzeit." You take the Stein to where you are working and take a swig whenever you can. Today Saturday 16th most of the stores displayed the following signs, "Die Kraft der Gemeinschaft ist unüberwindlich" (the power of the community is invincible).

Friday the 15th I noticed one of the columns in the paper describe Polish violations of Russian neutrality. Polish aeroplanes are reputed to have flown over Russian territory. It looks as if Russia is trying to build up a pretext for grabbing Ukraine. Poland has her hands too full to start antagonizing Russia.

Russia has taken Ukraine and White Russia. Saw "Westwall" in the movies for 20 pfg (cents). Tried it twice before but too many people were there that I thought I couldn't get in. First they showed a news short. The characteristic feature of this short was the hideous features of the Poles.

They all looked like criminals. They also showed a carload of Jews with long beards. When Hitler came on the screen nobody clapped or shouted approval or disapproval, which I have noticed in other movies already.

In the news short the Polish murderer who poked out the eyes of the German soldiers was shown on the screen. Comment among the people in the audience was audible. The Black Madonna of Poland, rather the Church where it is housed, was shown. Also about 15 German soldiers entering and then leaving the Church. As they left they put on their helmets, having evidently gone in to pray.

Then the distribution of food to the Poles was shown. Everywhere the German soldiers helped the Poles. Also the burning villages were shown which the commentator said were set on fire by the Poles.

The "Westwall" stressed the quantity of materials employed, the willingness of the workers and the speed with which it was finished. In contradistinction to France's Maginot Line, which being deep is claimed to be overflooded by the Rhine, the Westwall is built higher and is always dry.

On various street corners I noticed large placards reading SPIONAGE. In it instructions are given all German citizens to be aware of spies and how they must be handled.

FROM A YELLOW PAD OF PAPER—Not only were our ship tickets worthless but we also had purchased German rail tickets at reduced rates back home. We had planned to visit relatives of friends in Nünchritz, which lies near Leipzig in Saxony. Rather than let these go to waste, I decided to use them and made the trip to Leipzig.

There was no problem in the first leg of the trip, for the ticket was clearly printed from München nach Leipzig. However I had to use a similar ticket to return to Munich. I held my breath as the conductor perused my ticket. Fortunately he accepted it and I arrived safely in Munich.

FROM THE DIARY—Saturday night 23 Sept took the 10:30 train to

Leipzig. All shades were pulled down, and only dim blue lights shone in the coupes. For my companions I had a veterinarian who had studied in Munich and a woman traveler who also studied in Munich. The veterinarian said that his business was fairly good but that due to conditions in Germany it was better to spend the money in that a war was always liable to crop up. Both people were of the opinion that the war would last a while. I soon found from the tone of her conversation that she was anti-Nazi. My companion asked her if she was not afraid to ride with us. She replied "No," that she had ridden all over in trains even with the supposedly bestial Poles. At Hof the veterinarian alighted and both of us took advantage of this opportunity and stretched out on the seat, a European custom. Before I alighted in Leipzig, the woman told me that she sent all her friends in America, letters, telling them that the German people do not want the present war nor the present government. She said that I would notice that the people in Northern Germany were slaves and liked to be bossed.

In Leipzig, the largest railroad station, I ate breakfast—a terrible cup of coffee and was soon on my way to Reisa. From Reisa I walked to Nünchritz about 1 ¼ hours walk. Everywhere the people greet with "Heil Hitler," children on the street, elderly people, all. The walk to Nünchritz was very interesting as the entire distance was along the Elbe. Here I noticed that practically all children were very blonde. My friends said that these were all former fisherman's villages and that from these came the blondes.

Read good book in Nünchritz "Wetterzonen der Weltpolitik" (Weather zones of World Politics) by Pahl. Went into a Gasthaus that evening. Noticed a strange custom. A man came in and instead of shaking hands with his friends he rapped on the table. Then he went to another table. Sunday I left for Leipzig. Saw Völkerschlachdenkmal (the "Monument to the Battle of Nations" commemorates Napolean's defeat at Leipzig) a massive piece of architecture and Augustenplatz (home to the opera in Leipzig), largest of its kind in the world. Ate in the "Bärenschänke" evidently a "Studentenlokal" Poor meal—took midnight train to Munich and arrived at 8 o'clock the next morning. There had been Fliegeralarm (air raid siren) the previous night in Munich of which I had heard nothing in Leipzig. Even in Leipzig the people who entered the streetcar or waiting room in the station greeted with "Heil Hitler."

During the week heard that over a Swiss station it was reported that Julius Streicher was in Concentration Camp.

This previous sentence regarding Streicher, while untrue, points to the nature of the reporting in Germany at the time and a growing reliance on external, in this case, Swiss news. Julius Streicher was a staunch Nazi and follower of Adolf Hitler. In a periodical "Stürmer", Streicher continuously incited and encouraged anti-Semitic boycotts. Not only did the paper incite persecution, but also published the names of individual Jews, with their addresses, as suitable for victimization.[54]

Streicher was ultimately found guilty in Nuremberg of Crimes against Humanity and sentenced to death in October 1946. The judgment against him included:

"In his speeches and articles, week after week, month after month, he infected the German mind with the virus of anti-Semitism, and incited the German people to active persecution.... (his) incitement to murder and extermination at the time when Jews in the East were being killed under the most horrible conditions clearly constitutes the persecution on political and racial grounds in connection with war crimes, as defined by the Charter, and constitutes a crime against humanity."[55]

Part 3: Going Home

1939—TRAIN TO GENOA, MEETING A FREED PRISONER FROM DACHAU

FROM A YELLOW PAD OF PAPER—By the end of September, my funds had arrived from the States and I had to resign from the job. This entailed visiting the owner of the firm, Hans Moertelbauer. When I explained that I was returning to America, he said that I was lucky. He then pointed to a school across from his home. "See that school? Do you know what they teach there?" I of course had no idea. He continued, "They teach them how to break the windows of Jewish shops." I was flabbergasted that he would disclose his feelings about the regime to me, a perfect stranger.

This comment pointed to a high level of fear, similar to the conversation with the woman on the train to Leipzig. That one could have an opinion and express it to a perfect stranger, without fear of retaliation, was considered highly unusual.

Finally the time to make our departure had come. We took the train for Genoa. Only blue lights were lit in the train—Verdunkelung. However when we crossed the Brenner Pass into Italy, bright lights suddenly illuminated the train—Italy was not yet at war. We boarded the Italian liner "Rex" in Genoa and enjoyed Columbus Day, October 12, on the bounding main with plenty of pasta and vino rosso. We were stopped once by a French warship near Oran and again by a British ship near Gibraltar.

FROM THE DIARY—Tuesday evening at 7 o'clock boarded the train for Genoa. Just before we left, Frank Schoenberger showed me a card that he had received from a friend in the Chiemsee. It said that the party heard from reliable sources that the "Rex" would not sail. But inasmuch as we were all prepared, nobody thought of staying in Munich.

A Japanese delegation was escorted by German officials to a sleeping car on the same train. The train was crowded. Everything was dark save for a blue light. At 10:30 we arrived at the Brenner Pass. Already at Innsbruck an SS man entered and examined our passes for the "Ausreisesichtvermerk" (exit visa, travel approval.) One woman had to get off because she had none. At the Brenner we had to hand our passes and a Devisenschein (proof of currency note) to the Germans. No attempt was made to search for Devisen (currency) or even to look at the baggage because the train was too crowded. One woman came to Innsbruck via Stuttgart and had to have her entire baggage minutely examined.

We continued on into Italy after 1 ½ hours. Lights were put in the sockets as there is no Verdunklung (blackout) (as) in Germany.

About 10 o'clock we saw Genoa. It is a beautiful town laid on hills and mountains. We got a room on the waterfront "Alberger Porto Principe" for 25 L per person per day for board. The place was pretty dirty and the food not so extra good.

The next day we went to Campo Santo the famous cemetery. It is beautifully situated on the side of a hill. It consists of garden plots and huge hills with graves inserted in the sides of the walls. Here are to be found many wonderful works of architecture and sculpture. Thousands of tombs one on top of the other, on the steps everywhere. That night we walked through the town. Near the harbor the streets are narrow and the houses five to seven stories high. Wash is left hanging the whole night over these narrow streets and bats swoop down quite often. Innumerable bars and sailor hangouts are to be found here. Pissorts (public urinals) consist of a trough on the side of the wall often without any shelter in the back. These are quite frequent. The next day we got up early and went to the boat. On the pier we met an Austrian, ejected from Germany. After having served six months in Dachau he was told to leave. His wife and a 17-year-old son live in Vienna. He makes money on odd jobs, painting, etc. He was sending a letter to an uncle in America who has money but as yet has not offered to help him.

Dachau concentration camp was the first concentration camp in Germany, located in a suburb of Munich. It was opened in 1933 by Himmler. In the first year, the camp held about 4,800 prisoners and by 1937 the number had risen to 13,260. Initially the prisoners were German Communists, Social Democrats, and other opponents of the Nazi regime. The number of Jewish prisoners at Dachau rose with the increased persecution of the Jews and on November 10-11, 1938, in the aftermath of Kristallnacht, more than 10,000 Jewish men were interned there. Most of the men in this group were released after incarceration of a few weeks to a few months.[56]

From the ship's manifest from the Rex, George and his mother set sail on October 6, 1939 from Genoa to Naples to New York.

1939—SAILING HOME

FROM THE DIARY—The boat sailed at about 2 o'clock. The next morning, Saturday, we were already in Naples. I left the boat at 9 and wandered through the town. There are very many beggars and panhandlers in Italy. One fellow, a sailor from Palestine who could speak fairly fluent English told me to ride up the hill with a funicular railway. I did and was rewarded with a wonderful view of Vesuvius, the bay and the isle of Capri.

Got a shoeshine for one Lire and got on the boat at 11:30. At 1 o'clock we set sail again, hoping to reach New York.

FROM A YELLOW PAD OF PAPER—The first leg of my next visit to Germany was again on a liner, the RMS Queen Elizabeth, which served as a troopship for the American Army.

—George Beichl, 2005

5. Germany in 1945, as a Prisoner of War

FROM 1939 TO 1944 GEORGE CONTINUED HIS GRADUATE EDUCATION IN Chemistry at the University of Pennsylvania. When Japan bombed Pearl Harbor and the US entered the war in December 1941, WWII became a national priority. George watched as his friends and neighbors went off to war in Europe and the Pacific. Some became casualties, some went missing, and some came home battle-scarred. The increasing number of wounded and killed US soldiers meant that the Allies needed replacements. They needed Infantrymen more than they needed chemists, and they needed them badly. On July 10, 1944, George was inducted into the US Army and in December 1944, he was placed into the 4th Infantry Division, then in Luxembourg, as a replacement for the many killed and wounded in their recently completed fight in Germany's Hürtgen Forest.

While the exact date is unknown when George joined the 4th Infantry Division, the assumption is that he joined sometime in December 1944. A brief history of actions from December until the time he was captured in early February 1945 will provide a picture of actions George may have been involved in.

The 22nd Infantry Regiment of the 4th Infantry Division was withdrawn from the Hürtgen Forest on December 3, 1944 after suffering heavy casualties in their fight from November 16 to December 3, 1944. Most rifle companies in the regiment and the division suffered 150% casualties during that time period—many replacements were wounded as they moved up to join their company.

Moving to the relative quiet of Luxembourg, the division had a front line of over 35 miles that it was responsible for securing. With no activity of note from the Germans, the opportunity was taken for some men to take a three-day pass to Paris or another location in France for a break from the action. New men went through more training as they became accustomed to their new unit, old timers got their first shower in many days, and a time of rest, training, and resupply existed until that fateful date of December 16, 1944 when the final German blitz of the war began. Known in history as the Battle of the Bulge, the main German thrust hit in Belgium, north of the 4th Infantry Division's line. But to those who were there, the German attack into Luxembourg was equally as fierce. It became the responsibility of the division to hold the southern shoulder of the Bulge. While the 12th Infantry Regiment had the brunt of the fighting, George's Company E and the other companies of the 2nd Battalion, 22nd Infantry Regiment were called on to reinforce their sister regiment in the Luxembourg town of Osweiler, a fight which continued until it was secured just before Christmas.

The 4th Infantry Division held their line and blocked the German advance into Luxembourg. Later, General George Patton wrote to the division commander, "Your fight in the Hürtgen Forest was an epic of stark infantry combat; but, in my opinion, your most recent fight—from the 16th to the 26th of December—when, with a depleted and tired division, you halted the left shoulder of the German thrust into the American lines and saved the City of Luxembourg and the tremendous supply establishments and road nets in that vicinity, is the most outstanding accomplishment of yourself and your division."

As the Germans began to retreat, George and his fellow infantry soldiers held the line along the Luxembourg/German border as the war ground on into the new year of 1945. As the division moved back toward Belgium and the same place in the Siegfried Line they had breached in mid-September, the coldest winter in recent times gripped the countryside. Beginning in early February, George and the men of his regiment swept through the Siegfried Line and continued their intense pressure on the German army. Resistance increased as they fought on the

German homeland. George had no idea that he would soon be captured and become a Prisoner of War.

The dotted line represents the front line as of February 7 and the solid line represents the front line as of March 21, 1945. George was captured near Prüm, after a deadly siege that resulted in numerous casualties from his platoon. Battle lines in Germany were fluid and moved eastward. As the war shifted, so did the prisoners. As the Allies drew closer, some prisoners were released and others prisoners were put in boxcars and moved further east to established prison camps.

The After Action Reports from the 4th Infantry that day were as follows.[57]

8 FEBRUARY 1945: D+248 (AFTER ACTION REPORT)—Brig Gen Blakeley presented the DSC to Major Howard C Blazzard, 22nd Infantry. The enemy defended from hastily constructed field fortifications and from buildings. In the northern sector, the enemy offered slight resistance to the advance of CT 8, however, in the vicinity of Gondenbrett a more determined stand was made. CT 22 received three counterattacks during the period. All three attacks were against our forces in Obermehlen. The first two, which occurred at 0830 and 0910, consisted of an estimated company of infantry in each case. The third attack at 1030 was made up of tanks and infantry. All three attacks were repulsed without loss of ground. An unknown number of tanks were heard in the vicinity of Weinsheim at 1700. The Division gained very little ground during the day because of the increased amount of artillery, numerous small local counterattacks, and adverse weather conditions which resulted in very poor road conditions. The 8th Infantry continued the attack with the 1st Battalion on the right and the 3rd on the left. The 1st Battalion fought for the town of Gondenbrett throughout the day and succeeded in clearing all the town except for a few houses. The 2nd Battalion continued the advance and was on its objective by dark. The 3rd Battalion relieved the 2nd Battalion which moved to Washeid to reorganize. An increased amount of enemy artillery was reported during the latter part of the day. The 12th Infantry continued to hold favorable terrain on the right flank of the 8th Infantry before being relieved by the 8th Infantry. Then the 1st and 3rd Battalions of the 12th Infantry moved into position on the right flank of the Division. The 1st Battalion of the 22nd Infantry was relieved by this movement at 1915. The attack of the 22nd Infantry Regiment with the 2nd and 3rd Battalions began at 1300. The 2nd Battalion after repulsing several small counterattacks cleared the town of Obermehlen.

George explained that on the day his platoon was preparing for battle, they were digging foxholes in the frozen earth. The mood was solemn and quiet. All of a sudden, the Sergeant ran towards them yelling, "Get the hell out of here!" Immediately their blood started pumping. The soldiers grabbed their weapons and dashed into the forest following the footsteps of the Sergeant. The approaching Germans were unabashed in their mission to demolish the platoon. They held nothing back and were aggressively shooting both machine guns and missiles into the forest at a fever pitch. George was relatively certain he would be killed. His daughter relayed this story:

FROM GEORGE'S DAUGHTER—But it was not until my dad was in his 80s that he told me something else about that time. He explained to me that as the shots and missiles entered the forest, he thought of his mother alone in Philadelphia and prayed to God that if he could live, he would pray a rosary[58] a day for the rest of his life.

He kept diving for cover over trees that were being knocked down in front of him. "I didn't think it could possibly get worse," he said. Then, after an extended pause, he continued, "But it did."

He made himself an easy target by climbing over felled trees. The bullets hit his fellow soldiers to his left and his right. Missiles blew up in front of and behind him. The powerful sounds of exploding artillery and the horrific and despairing screams and cries of the petrified, wounded and dying men must have been horrifying.

And I had the image of my dad, desperate to survive. I thought of the powerful stench of heavy artillery hitting its intended targets, the blood, the smoke, the fire, the death, the anger, the fear, the fallout.

When my dad recognized that the odds of surviving were impossible, he changed his mind.

"I then promised to pray two rosaries a day," he continued, "for the rest of my life."

I was astounded.

All the years I had known my dad, all the things we had talked about, and yet never once did he mention this to me, not until he was in his late 80's?

He explained that he kept that promise until sometime in the late 1970s, when life got so busy for him that he found praying two rosaries a day difficult to maintain. He was grateful to the Lord for saving his life and took his promise of two rosaries a day very seriously. It was a genuine dilemma. Unsure how best to proceed, he spoke to a Jesuit priest, explained the situation, and requested special dispensation to return to one rosary a day.

It was granted.

I was puzzled as to why he only told me this now, so late in his life, and when I asked him, he merely shrugged his shoulders.

At the edge of the forest he could see a clearing. As he crawled out of the smoke filled forest, there were a few German foot soldiers with guns poised waiting for him.

He never said what happened next.

FROM A MEMOIR OF A CLOSE FRIEND—"George was working at St. Joe's and getting a master's degree in Chemistry. Despite his severe astigmatism and absolute near sightedness, he was still, by some fluke, drafted later on in the War. He was sent into the infantry and during the heavy fighting in Germany, George's platoon was captured by the Germans. This was scary. He understood the Germans, but he had to pretend he did not know German. Fortunately the Germans knew they were defeated and they did not kill the members of the platoon."[59]

*

The casualties in the forest were significant that day, so much so that George was reported "Killed in Action." His name was listed in the Philadelphia Inquirer under "casualties."

But he was still very much alive.

Casualties

28 Men Killed, 39 Are Wounded

Twenty-eight men from the Philadelphia area have been killed, six are reported missing and 39 have been wounded in action, according to War and Navy Department casualty lists released yesterday and notifications to next of kin.

Less than three weeks after arriving overseas, Private First Class George J. Beichl, 26, former professor of chemistry at St. Joseph's College, was reported killed in action in Germany with the infantry, his mother, Mrs. Louisa Beichl, of 1430 N. Dover st., was notified by the War Department.

Private Beichl entered the Army last Aug. 9, went overseas last

P. F. C. BEICHL month. A graduate of St. Joseph's High School and College in the classes of 1935 and 1939, respectively, he took his Master's Degree in chemistry at the

University of Pennsylvania. He was a member of the St. Joseph's faculty since 1939.

*

George was captured in February 1945 and was extremely fortunate to be alive, particularly given the Nazi massacre of captured American soldiers that occurred less than two months before in Malmédy. The Malmédy Massacre in Belgium (December 1944) was the brazen murder of more than 80 American GIs who surrendered to their German captors, not realizing they were dealing with the SS ("Schutzstaffel" or Protection Squad), specifically the Kampfgruppe (Attack Group) Peiper[60] (part of the SS Panzer Division later tried for war crimes).

The captured American GIs were marched to a nearby field and the SS commander ordered a mass execution.[61] Survivors of the initial execution were killed by a pistol shot to the head, in some cases by an English speaking SS soldier who was said to have walked among the survivors, asking if anyone was hurt. If anyone responded in the affirmative, he was shot in the head.[62] The SS were notorious in their shameless and unadulterated violence, and this was not the first nor the last massacre of this type for them. After the SS troops moved on, the few remaining soldiers reported the massacre. News spread very quickly among the troops that Germans were shooting prisoners of war. When knowledge of the massacre spread, there was retaliation against German prisoners of war.[63]

Fortunately for George, there were no Nazi SS troops nearby during the battle at Prüm. The anxious prisoners were taken to Wittlich Prison. The estimated time to walk from Prüm to Wittlich was anywhere from 10 to 12 hours. Eventually, George was moved to Stalag XIIA.

Both the Wittlich Prison and Stalag XIIA in Limburg were work camps where prisoners were able to leave for portions of the day under guard and perform work duties, hoping not to get hit by aerial bombs or explosions. The Allies were not always discriminating in their targets, which sometimes included prison camps and marked and unmarked trains hauling prisoners, taking the lives of bystanders, friends and foes alike.

Germany signed the Geneva Convention (Japan did not, and the prisoners of war captured in the Pacific had a horrific time with a death rate of over 40%).[64] The Geneva Convention was a series of treaties agreed upon in terms of the treatment of civilians and prisoners of war.[65] It provided, for example, that boxcars carrying prisoners should carry fixed and distinctive markings to prevent the Allies from bombing their own. However, on most occasions in the diary, George and fellow prisoners were transported in unmarked boxcars. The Geneva Convention also provided that a prisoner's personal possessions, other than arms and horses, must not be taken from them.

Germany and Italy generally treated the POWs from France, US and the British Commonwealth according to the convention. Germans were obliged to treat Jewish POWs in Allied uniforms the same as the other prisoners, though that did not always occur. An estimated 350 American GI POWs who were Jewish or suspected of being Jewish were sent to labor camps by Germans during WWII and about 20% of them died in captivity.[66]

And while we know that George initially hid his ability to speak

German fluently, we also know that his personal health was deteriorating and that at some point he decided to communicate in German.

George always asked for what he needed. And in that moment when he decided it was time to ask for help, he had to consider his options very carefully. He contemplated which of the German guards might help him, which one might be sympathetic to the human condition.

A German-speaking American prisoner was more than just an enemy to the German soldiers; he was a traitor. In their eyes, George carried the same blood and culture in his veins, yet he denied it in loyalty to a foreign government. He was willing to kill fellow brothers and kinsman for a country that was a melting pot of immigrants and for a cause of freedom. For a German-speaking American prisoner to have the nerve to ask a German guard at a prison camp for personal help required enormous confidence. Any guard helping a prisoner was risking his own life.

The specific guard George approached, Karl Schäfer, did just that. It is unclear where the discussions took place or how the arrangement was made, but Karl and his wife Gretel openly risked their lives and secretly shared what meager provisions they had with George. This included bread, herbs, tea, and anything they could think of that might improve his physical health.

The Schäfer's secretly left the spare provisions for George out in the fields where he was working. They had to be extremely careful about where they left the tea and herbs, but once they realized that it worked, they continued to help him for as long as he was kept in the Wittlich Prison.

George often said, "If it wasn't for Karl, I would not have survived, I was really very sick."

And over time, the bread and tea and herbs left in the fields restored him to health. And throughout his life he would remark, "It was the best bread I ever had."

THE TRANSLATOR

When George's fluency was discovered in the Wittlich Prison, it became an advantage. He was able to help explain work details, or assist in any translation issues that emerged. So when his fellow prisoners wanted more food, for example, they sent him in to negotiate.

On the other hand, his German fluency had the staunch German soldiers angrily contemplating exactly *why* he wasn't fighting on their side. And they considered just what to do about it.

A FRIENDSHIP

Karl and George became friends. Over time, they talked about more than just physical symptoms and hunger. As George's health improved, their conversations moved to different topics. George learned that Karl had been in the infantry, fighting in Russia. He was sent home due to frostbite and other injuries, but was required to work at the Wittlich Prison, which was close to his family in Trier. Through these conversations, George also learned that Karl was an artist who loved to paint and draw the countryside. They often talked about historical Trier, Karl's home city. Trier is also home to the Porta Nigra, a beautiful piece of Roman architecture, and this led to discussions about architecture and the Holy Roman Empire.

FROM GEORGE'S DAUGHTER—There was a small drawing of the Porta Nigra on my dad's bedroom wall. In fact, it sat there in the middle of the main wall for as long as I can remember. I later learned that Karl drew this picture and gave it to my dad as a way to remember that time and place. And my dad kept it and framed it and looked at it daily.

For most of my life I did not know who Karl Schäfer was, and I had no idea about their history, that he and my dad spent time talking about both the Porta Nigra and Roman architecture. With a background of artillery firing and crumbling buildings, it must have been a dramatic contrast.

TRIER Porta-Nigra

And because George could speak and read German, to pass the time, Karl provided him with a book, "Das Flammende Wort" *(The Flaming Word)*. The book itself is a novel about Germany's first journalist, Christian Friedrich Daniel Schubart, but it also became his diary.

6. 1945 Diary—Introduction

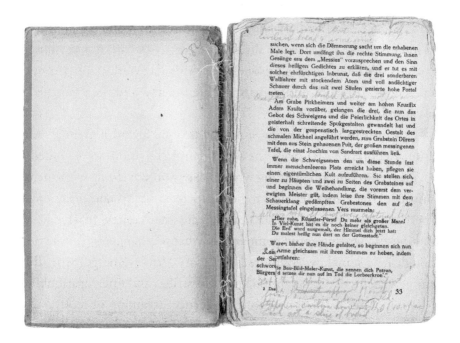

GEORGE KEPT THIS DIARY, WRITTEN IN ENGLISH, IN THE TOP DRAWER OF the big metal desk that sat in his study on Drexel Road in Overbrook, Pennsylvania.

The diary itself starts on page 31. The missing pages were used as toilet paper and, as he explained, he was urged to "read faster" so his fellow prisoners could have access to the pages. The first date mentioned is February 12, 1945. The words are written in faded pencil around the edges of the brittle pages and it's difficult to read even with a powerful magnifying glass or two. He jotted thoughts and snippets of information from the events unfolding in front of him. Sometimes it is hard to follow the flow of words. Often simple phrases like "During Mass we had to hit floor several times due to close bombing by our planes," and "Taken to castle where I was interrogated" stand in stark contrast to the gravity of the content. He writes about "delousing" with regularity, of the cold, of the hunger, and yet he enjoys singing with fellow prisoners, learning Russian chemistry terms, and finds joy in his friendship with the prison guard Schäfer. In this diary there are mentions of stopping in a house for some bread, or someone sharing a beer. These are not commonly associated with the life of a prisoner. But this was a work camp. Prisoners were sent out to work under guard during the day, and then returned to the camp in the evening.

The words in the following indented text are all from George. After Action Reports (AAR) from the 4th Infantry Division are included to provide some context regarding what his division was doing while he was a prisoner. There are references to newspapers, thoughts and commentary in between his writing in an attempt to create some context to what he was thinking and writing about compared to what was happening at the time. Though it is somehow disjointed, the story clearly emerges with three common themes: hunger and sickness, air strikes and interrogations, and liberation. And his responses to these events: dreaming of food, feeling fortunate, prayer, and gratitude.

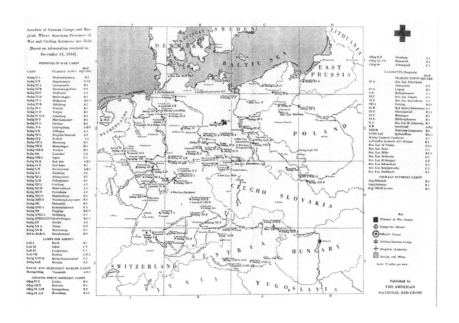

Part 1: Arrival

1945—STALAG XIIA
7 DAYS AFTER BEING CAPTURED

The following passage is from *The Pegasus Archive*.

Conditions at Limburg were notoriously bad with next to nothing in the way of facilities. This is partly explained by the fact that Stalag XIIA's primary function was to act as a transit camp that processed newly captured Prisoners of War before distributing them amongst the other, better-organized Stalags in Germany. Typically a new prisoner would arrive, be interrogated, documented, and moved on within a few weeks; therefore most men did not have to endure this depressing camp for long. However it was as a consequence of this short stay that the prisoners could not be organized to make the conditions more habitable, nor were new arrivals able to receive in such a short period of time the luxuries of the frequently life-saving Red Cross parcels. The population of the camp was always extremely high because for many prisoners captured on the Western Front, passing through the gates of Stalag XIIA was their first point of call.

For the British and Americans, temporary accommodation came in the form of four very large marquees, not wholly dissimilar to circus tents. There was no furniture of any kind inside these structures, instead the cramped conditions dictated that everyone had to sleep back to back on the floor, which in some instances was cobbled stone, with, if they were extremely lucky, a loose scattering of straw for bedding.

Between meals, which were only a few notches above starvation rations, there was absolutely nothing in the way of entertainment to occupy the minds of the prisoners. There was no lighting in the camp, and so as soon as it got dark men slept until dawn because there was little point to being awake. The threat of disease, especially diarrhea, was far from being uncommon, and the camp possessed almost nothing in the way of medical facilities. The stone toilets served several thousand men, and as such created a considerable stench.

Despite the transitory nature of the camp, some of those held at Stalag XIIA were more permanent residents and spent several years there. The Russians were, as was the case in all German camps, treated as a sub-species and were effectively left to rot. However there was a sizeable population of Indian soldiers who had been captured during the fighting in North Africa in 1942, and they sat out the remainder of the war at Limburg. As Commonwealth troops they were treated better than most, and like POW's all over Germany who had been imprisoned for a long time, they had learned how to make their lives reasonably comfortable and were able to keep both themselves and their quarters clean.

Upon arrival, men who were newcomers to life as a POW had the basic ground rules of Stalag law spelled out to them, one of which was a warning that they would be shot if they placed as much as a finger upon the tall barbed wire fence that surrounded the camp. For many freshly captured servicemen, Stalag XIIA was their first opportunity to write a postcard home to their family, and although it would take weeks to arrive, it was often the case that this would be the first news they would receive that their loved ones, now posted as missing-in-action, were alive.

Prisoner of War Camp

STALAG XIIA

Date MARCH 8, 1945

(No. of Camp only; as may be directed by the Commandant of the Camp.)

I have been taken prisoner of war in Germany. I am in good health — slightly wounded (cancel accordingly).

We will be transported from here to another Camp within the next few days. Please don't write until I give new address.

Kindest regards

Christian Name and Surname: GEORGE BEICHL

Rank: PRIVATE

Detachment: US ARMY

(No further details. — Clear legible writing.)

There were a total of 58,000 men interred at Stalag XIIA,[67] an estimated 15,000 (26%) of them Americans.[68]

1945—KARL SCHÄFER

FROM THE DIARY—February 12—Krötz in Wittlich on house-building detail. Got word from bombed slaughterhouse. Drank wine. Didn't like clear weather because that meant Jabos *(fighter bombers).*[69] We were afraid of them since they would attack anything that moved. We would always look for cover when we were out in the open in case Jabos appeared.

A Supermarine Spitfire Mk. IX in Longues-sur-Mer, Normandy (1944). It carries a 500 lb bomb under the fuselage and a 250 lb bomb under each wing. Pilot Officer Saidman, Royal Air Force official photographer. This is photograph CL 726 from the collections of the Imperial War Museums

Went to side of hill where lady had her vineyard. Helped build shanty. Karl Schäfer—Constructor. His house in Trier had been destroyed. Released from *(German)* army because of frostbite and other injuries he suffered in Russia.

I had been captured in the vicinity of Prüm and had been brought with others to a civilian prison in Wittlich.

Some fellows worked in vineyard pruning vines.

*

The **After Action Reports** throughout this section describe what George's division was doing around the same time as the diary entry, allowing a comparison of his life to the rest of his fellow soldiers.

4TH INFANTRY DIVISION AFTER ACTION REPORT—15 February 1945 - D+255[70] A letter was received from VIII Corps authorizing an allotment of British Awards and Decorations. The enemy continued to defend the same line and sent patrols west of this line in order to probe our positions to determine strength and disposition. The 4th Infantry Division continued to organize and defend within its sector. Forward elements received intermittent artillery fire throughout the period.

FROM THE DIARY—Got warm soup and civilian bread and some wine. One day Jabo *(fighter bomber)* bombed railway not far away. Two fellows took off but were captured later. Schäfer thinks Yanks not as good infantry as Heinies *(slang term for a German from the name Heinrich. The meaning "buttocks" emerged in the 1920s and is probably unrelated, a modification of 'behind.')*.[71] Mentioned the strafing *(repeated aircraft attacks with bombs or machine-gun fire)* of civilian homes such as in Wittlich. Nevertheless a well-meaning fellow and a good boss. Most people ask us what we Americans want in Europe. Most treat us kindly.

Boeing B-17F bombing through overcast Bremen, Germany, 13 November 1943

1945—INITIAL INTERROGATION, WALKING AND HUNGER

FROM THE DIARY—February 18 Sunday walked 10 miles to load wood in rain. Caught cold. Stopped in civilian home for H2O (10 of us). Each got a slice of bread. All ask me naturally where I learned German. Most agree that there is nothing that one can do about the draft. They say that it is the same with them. Strangely enough the 1st question all ask me when interrogated is if I was a volunteer. Back in Prüm or Rollersheim where I spent the first night one German major commented in English, "Very Sad." A German General asked me, "Are you German or American?" When I said the latter he said, "And your mother is Austrian?"

Hitler was born in Austria.

Sick all week of the 18th GI's *(gastrointestinal disorders)* and no appetite. Given Tannelbin and opium.

1945—KEEPING COMPANY WITH THE "ENEMY"— GETTING A HAIRCUT

4TH INFANTRY DIVISION AFTER ACTION REPORT: 19 FEBRUARY 1945 TO D+259—The enemy continued to employ harassing small arms, artillery and mortar fire. Noise of tracked vehicles was heard on the Weinsheim-Dausfeld road between 0300 and 0400. The 4th Division continued on a defensive mission while the remainder of VIII Corps continued the attack against the Siegfried Line. Active patrolling was conducted by the infantry regiments and ambush patrols were established on the west bank of the Prüm river.

FROM THE DIARY—Monday Feb 19th Although sick reported with Clairmont for house detail. Told Schäfer. He took me to his house and gave me a couple of shots of Hefferl, a whiskey made from Mosel wine. He also had his wife make me an herb tea which she brought out to the house in a Thermos bottle. Very bitter—cammomile, peppermint and vermouth. Also Glühwein… didn't help however since I must have had an intestinal infection. Later he took us to a neighboring shanty where he gave us a badly needed haircut. Here we were entertained by a young German sailor on leave. Played modern tunes on accordion. "Ferry Band Serenade" he knew as an Italian number. Also the Woodpecker which I first heard in "Rex."

Sailors have plenty to eat and drink. Father (45 years old) a soldier was also on leave preliminary to going on the Front. Next day we did not go on House detail because Frau Krötz was over and Schäfer did not personally appear at the Lager to ask for us.

Gave most of my bread and soup away. Could eat the bread if toasted since it took the sogginess out of it. (We toasted the bread on a pot-belly stove in our room)[72]

Here was our menu and schedule. 7 am Aufstehen *(get up)*. 2 Mann Kaffee holen *(2 men get coffee)*. Everybody ran for that detail for it presented an opportunity to steal some carrots or potatoes from kitchen. 4 men to a short loaf of sourdough bread. Those who worked on Friedhof Komando *(cemetery detail)* 3 men to a loaf.

Small pad of oleo *(margarine)* to each man and on Thursdays and Sundays we got 1 plate of molasses syrup to 10 men. That amounted to a tablespoon and a half of syrup.

11:30 AM Suppe- Potato or Cabbage soup. Often had seconds.

4:30PM Suppe—ditto

Sundays we got potatoes and gravy for supper. Got potatoes and carrots on sly from kitchen or from Victory Gardens *(Schrebegärten)*. Guards exchanged a loaf of bread for galoshes or fountain pens. They also offered leaf tobacco. Many traded sweaters.

1945—CONTINUING TO WORK, NO MORE NAZI PARADING

4TH INFANTRY DIVISION AFTER ACTION REPORT: 26 FEBRUARY 1945 TO D+266—Opposite CT 12 and 22 the enemy remained wholly defensive. Stray aggressive enemy patrols operated in the central and southern part of CT 8's sector. Considerable vehicular movement to the east tended to substantiate the belief that some elements opposite the 4th

Infantry Division were being relieved. The 12th and 22nd Regiments reported that the enemy was unusually quiet along the entire sector.

FROM THE DIARY—February 26th Went on cemetery detail. Some dug, others filled up holes while others graded. We dug one long trench. That day we witnessed a German Military funeral. Body had been interred previously. Catholic Chaplain in German uniform. 12 soldiers in faded uniforms gave rifle salute. Some were green, gray and one wore a black Panzer jacket. What a change from the old days of Nazi parading. Chaplain blessed grave and gave brief sermon on the "Dust to Dust" theme also stressing the need of courage for the remaining relatives.

We worked in WPA style. An Italian detail also there worked much harder than we. Buried 3 men a Russian, Jugoslav, and GI a Marvin Gold from Pittsburgh. Bodies naked were placed in sack and put in the trench and covered with dirt. Quit around 1pm walked through bombed streets of Wittlich to Lager. Practically all stores in town were a mass of rubble.

WPA style refers to the Works Progress Administration (WPA) style of taking the general unemployed population to carry out public work projects. In this case, the German Army was using their prisoners to help them carry out their local projects.

When asked towards the end of his life if he knew the GI he buried, George shook his head no.

1945—THE DAILY LIFE OF A PRISONER

4TH INFANTRY DIVISION AFTER ACTION REPORT: 27 FEBRUARY 1945 TO D+267—The enemy continued to maintain its hastily prepared line of field fortifications with no aggressive action. At this time it was believed that the 5th Para Division with a total estimated strength of 1000 men constituted the opposition in the 4th Infantry Division zone. All three regiments sent out two patrols each at 0300 to contact the enemy as diversionary demonstration for the 87th Infantry Division attack (despite the fact that the attack had finally occurred at 1500 on February 26.) During the day, the VIII Corps issued a field order which required the 4th Division to launch an attack to the east on February 28 at 0515. The 8th and 22nd Regiments conducted extensive reconnaissance in preparation for the attack. Elements of the 12th Infantry were relieved by the 6th Armored Division during the night of 27-28 February. The 12th Infantry in turn relieved the 2nd Battalion of the 22nd Infantry Regiment in the vicinity of Prüm. As soon as the 6th Armored Division and the 22nd Infantry progressed sufficiently to cover the front of the present defensive position, the 12th Infantry was to assemble in division reserve.

FROM THE DIARY—Feb 27 Pumped water. Met among Prisoners, 1 man sentenced to 17 months for Schwarzschlacht. i.e., slaughtering pig without permission. Another 2 years for saying that the news that 35 ships were sunk in North Atlantic was a lie. Many Russians also here.

No talk of women, only food. I dream of chocolate cake and ice cream every night—and enjoy it.

Some of the men went into town on a work detail. Also some books. They got from a bombed house. One was Meister Eckhardt's "Reden der Unterweisungen" I also had Lukas Hain by Tinhofer, donated by Schäfer. I suspected that Meister Eckhart was on the Index. At Limburg, the American chaplain *(also a Prisoner of War there)*, a New Yorker who had Fr. O'Brien S.J. as high school instructor, suggested I scrap it, so before finishing it, it became toilet paper. But I find that in 1329 a papal condemned many books of Eckhart's theses.

The publisher lauds Eckhart for his German concept of God dwelling within us. His treatment of sin is peculiar and was specifically condemned. "He who may have incorporated himself into God's will, he should not want at all—überhaupt—that the sins into which he had fallen had not occurred. His God is a God of the present and does not demand any trembling penitential humbling if only the man will turn to the Good within his heart."

1945—EXPERIENCING HUNGER, WALKING, BEER

4TH INFANTRY DIVISION AFTER ACTION REPORT: 28 FEBRUARY 1945 TO D+268—Notes about logistics: The road net within the division and VIII Corps sector continued to deteriorate rapidly because of the sudden thaw and because of extremely heavy traffic. As one road broke down, traffic was diverted to alternate roads which became progressively worse. In some cases it was necessary to remove the rails from railroad beds and utilize these roadbeds for vehicular traffic. Traffic was held to a minimum, only supply and other essential vehicles, and the speed limit was reduced to 15 miles per hour for all vehicles. To further reduce the burden of the road network and to facilitate the supply of the division units, service elements were moved forward rapidly. Because of the rapid advance of the enemy in their breakthrough of December, great quantities of material of all types had been abandoned throughout the entire area. An extensive salvage program was initiated and large quantities of ammunition and equipment were recovered. Numerous dead, both friendly and enemy, which had been left by troops formerly in the area were also discovered.

FROM THE DIARY—Feb 28th Wednesday left Wittlich around 7pm- about 25 of us and 3 guards and 1 loaf of bread and ¼ pound of sausage. Roads crowded with trucks and refugees. In day time few trucks abroad. Walked 4 km to neighboring town. Here we stayed in station room until 3:30 AM when our train arrived due at 8PM night before. Rode in the windowless compartment (glass panes all broken) for about 20 KM to Minderich.

End of line. Walked along Moselle and then through a tunnel which brought us to bridge about the size of the Girard Avenue Bridge over the Schuylkill. It had been bombed in center but some of the travelers climbed right over the top to the split and then passed on to lower platforms. Our guards would not risk it. Some walked 10 to 12 KM along left bank of Moselle passing thru every scenic town.

We had missed the only train. So nothing to do but wait until next day. We reached Eller where we stayed for a while in Railroad tunnel. This was Thursday Mar 1. It was plenty cold so we walked through the tunnel 4 KM to Cochem. Here also everything was destroyed i.e., no place to warm oneself up. Had we taken the auto road it would have taken 27 KM. We stayed at the other end of tunnel all day. Dobruky spoke to some Poles who gave us tobacco. All trains were kept in tunnels during the day. Poles and Russians worked on the railroads. Some German soldiers gave us beer.

These random experiences demonstrate unexpected camaraderie between enemies.

That night we tried to get a hop in the same old drizzling rain. Many trucks, many refugees, old and young, male and female. After an hour we recognized the futility of it and went back to the tunnel. We stayed in a boxcar til next morning at 5:00 AM. We then walked to station along the tracks bathed by a clear bright moon. Huddled in the shadow of the already bombed station we waited a ½ hour for train while a house was blazing away 1 block from station. Glad to get train and get away.

This train also had every window blown out and also quite crowded.

Finally reached Koblenz around 7AM. The town was leveled. Stayed in Bunker hewn out of rock. Air raids practically all day filled up the bunker which was pretty cold and draughty.

"Bundesarchiv Bild 146-1970-088-56, Koblenz, Ruinen Am Plan" by
US Signal Corps—Deutsches Bundesarchiv (German Federal Archive),
Bild 146-1970-088-56.

4TH INFANTRY DIVISION CASUALTIES FOR THE MONTH OF FEBRUARY 1945

KILLED IN ACTION: 15 officers, 255 enlisted
MISSING IN ACTION: 1 officer, 76 enlisted
SERIOUSLY WOUNDED IN ACTION: 10 officers, 95 enlisted
LIGHTLY WOUNDED IN ACTION: 50 officers, 847 enlisted

TOTAL CASUALTIES: 76 officers, 1,273 enlisted

Part 2: Settling In

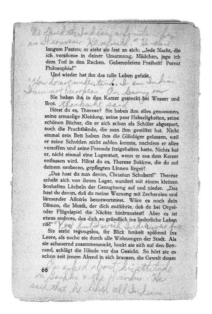

FROM THE DIARY—During air raid all types of people came in Russians, Poles, French and even some British Indians.

These were Mohammedans and had quite difficulty in speaking English. They had been captured in Italy. They asked us where English were fighting. They dislike England greatly and ask what America's attitude to India is?

They gave us cigarettes, a can of pineapple, chocolate, cake from their Red Cross rations. They also brought us some stew. Poles brought us beer. We could stand those rations.

When Britain declared war on Germany in September 1939, India was occupied by the British. Britain entered into war without consulting India, yet it required masses of Indians to fight on Britain's behalf. The British Indian Army began with 200,000 soldiers in 1939 and increased to over 2.5 million men by August 1945.[73] Indian soldiers fought with distinction and earned 30 Victoria Crosses (for demonstrating bravery) during WWII.[74] Though Indian soldiers fought nobly for the British Commonwealth, many would have preferred fighting for India's freedom from Britain instead.

Within India there were factions that supported the British war effort and some that did not. Mahatma Gandhi (part of the Congress leadership), for example, believed in non-violent resistance.[75] He launched a civil disobedience campaign calling for Independence from Britain in August 1942 called the "Quit India Movement" (Bharat Chhodo Andolan, or the August Movement).[76] Another important figure in India's WWII history was Subhas Chandra Bose. Bose wrote "The Indian Struggle, 1920-1934" and was a fierce advocate of a free India. In 1941 he fled to Germany to gain support for India's fight for freedom from British rule.[77] With Germany's help he recruited Indian soldiers from the Prisoner of War camps into the "Free India Legion."[78] In August 1942, an estimated 3,000 Indian POW volunteers made oaths of allegiance to Adolf Hitler.[79] Unfortunately, after Germany's stunning defeat in Stalingrad in February 1943, Bose recognized Germany would not be in a position to help free India, so he left for Japan, where he recruited 60,000 men to march on India.[80]

The "Free India Legion" that Bose organized in Germany was then drafted into Himmler's Waffen SS. Shortly before Germany surrendered in 1945, troops of the "Free India Legion" marched to Switzerland, a neutral country. They were refused entry, captured by the Allies and sent back to India.

General Field Marshal Erwin Rommel inspecting a unit of the Indian
Legion in France, February 1944
Bundesarchiv, Bild 183-J16796 / CC-BY-SA

We offered the Indian a fountain pen as a souvenir. He refused. He
said, "You do not understand. I am Indian I am not European." On
hearing our thanks he said, "Yes, but I wish India were free." (When)
asked about his attitude on Gandhi and the Hindus, he said that he liked
all Indians. Communal disturbances he attributed to British interference.

The Indians worked on a graveyard detail but due to frequent raids
spent most of the day in the Bunker.

This Jerry *(slang for German soldier)*—around 50 years old—said that
he had been drafted to work in Koblenz for 3 Marks per day although
he owned a farm on which he paid a Polish girl 4 Marks per day. He said
that he would be released when farming season started.

1945—TRAVELING, AIR RAID SIRENS

FROM THE DIARY—Met a German who predicted Yanks would be in
Koblenz by 2 weeks. We all laughed since everyone predicted a speedy
end. They all ask why are Americans so slow?

Civilian mentioned that Dec 23 night bomber attacked PW camp and killed 80 American officers.

Indians told us that Turkey had declared war on Germany and would relieve Russia on the Hungarian front. Got on train at 6:30 PM. It was supposed to pull out by 7PM but an air raid alert intervened.

In June 1940, Turkey announced neutrality. The geography of the country put it in a precarious position, with the Soviet Union on one side and Axis powers on two other sides. By February 23 1945, Turkey, anticipating Hitler's defeat, declared war on Germany and Japan.[81] *This action sanctioned Turkey's entry into the United Nations. "..only those states which had, by March 1945, declared war on Germany and Japan and subscribed to the United Nations Declaration, were invited to take part."*[82]

The United Nations declaration aimed to create an alliance that was outlined in the Atlantic Charter.

The Atlantic Charter was created in 1941 (when the Axis powers were still increasing) between President Roosevelt and Prime Minister Churchill. The Charter affirmed "certain common principles in the national policies of their respective countries on which they based their hopes for a better future for the world."[83]

The sixth clause of the Atlantic Charter states "After the final destruction of Nazi tyranny, they hope to see established a peace which will afford all nations the means of dwelling in safety within their own boundaries, and which will afford assurance that all men in the lands may live out their lives in freedom from fear and want."[84]

The League of Nations was established at the end of WWI "to promote international cooperation and to achieve peace and security." The League of Nations terminated activities after failing to prevent WWII, and would be replaced by The United Nations.[85]

No tickets were required in these trains and no conductor or ticket officers.

Soldiers usually with full field pack.

Refugees, men and women laden with rucksacks, etc.

We got out of wagon and ran underneath trucks. When Vollalarm sounded we ran up and over a bridge into bunker. Fortunately no bombs fell on Koblenz, because we were in center of bridge when planks were overhead.

After ½ hour, Vorentwarnung allowed us to return to train but lack of locomotive delayed our departure until 10PM. Big sign in station "Qualmen Verboten" (Smoking forbidden)

Locomotives seek train sheds during raid and they need time to get up steam.

At midnight we reach Andernach which had been bombed that day. All passengers for Cologne had to alight there also.

On one of bombed buildings stood a white painted word TROTZDEM *(in spite of this)*

The "Vollalarm" and the "Vorentwarnung" are part of the siren package. Air raid sirens consisted of held tones, "Vollalarm" lasting about 5 to 6 seconds each. These signals indicated that there was clear and distinct bombing. When the air danger had passed, there was the "Vorentwarnung" signal, which was a series of three held siren sounds in a row.

Every time planes overhead we sought cover under trees.

Walked 5 miles to deserted Miesenheim, a quiet, peaceful country town. Chimes on church steeple announced 1 o'clock.

1945 ZIGZAG TRENCHES IN A PEACEFUL TOWN

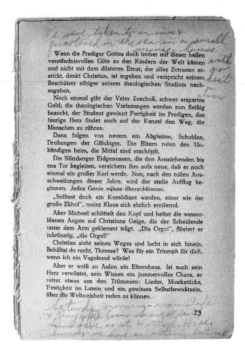

FROM THE DIARY—We were taken to an inn and quartered in the rear in a small movie house with no heat or straw.

Saturday morning marmalade and Jerry coffee (sans sucre et lait) *(without sugar and cream)*. Same fare as at Wittlich. Here, however, we have an outside latrine. Cleanest and most peaceful town yet. Worked on Splitershutzgraben in afternoon—long zigzag trench.

Trench warfare refers to fighting from trenches dug into the ground. During WWI, there were trench lines dug in a zig zag fashion, essentially breaking the trench into sections, so that, for example, an enemy could not shoot down the trench and directly hit combatants.

An additional advantage was that if a bomb landed in the trench, the blast was somewhat controlled.[86]

Ground is black and loose, easiest digging yet experienced. Many school children came to watch us. "Have you Schokolade *(chocolate)*?" they would ask. Of course we had none. We asked them for apples and they promised us some the next day.

Guards claim Cologne about finished. Other GI's coming in from work camps—ousted by Yanks. Yanks close to Wittlich. Many transports to Limburg but not for me yet.

1945 RELIGION AND WAR

FROM THE DIARY—Sunday March 4. Asked one of the German non-coms if we would have the opportunity to attend Mass. He replied that he would attend Church after the war and not during. How can one pray with a rosary in one hand and a gun to kill someone in the other?

Went on an 8 man detail to nearby Horse Hospital, Pferdelazarett. All had been given at least 1 Begasung *(form of anesthesia)* treatment. Our job was to clean them with straw due to lack of curvy combs. Then we unloaded hay from an overturned wagon which was result of runaway.

German guards did more work than we. They realized that they will surrender the PWs and are philosophical about that.

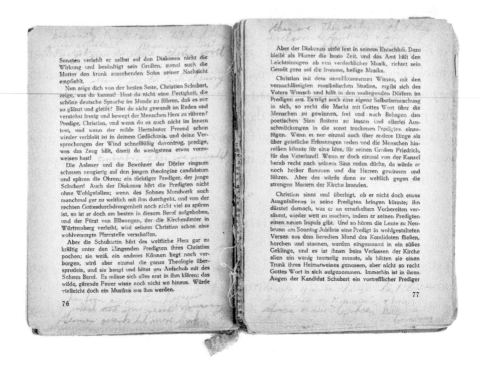

1945—CASUALTIES OF WAR

FROM THE DIARY—The non-com in charge had lost 2 brothers in Russia and 1 in Africa and mother had been killed in bombing. Yet he was thankful that his wife and child were still alive. His only wish was that the war would end soon.

While we were bumming a German major (in a one horse shay) entered and saw the Tankers working. He gave instructions that the PWs were to do the work, the Germans to direct us, but they disregarded that.

Signs of deterioration among the ranks

FROM THE DIARY—Met French and Poles digging bunkers in side of hill. All predicted end to war 2 to 3 weeks. Some Polish women also worked. They lived in neighboring towns. Gave us tobacco and apples. On way home we met a Polish woman and 2 children who gave us again apples and tobacco.

Some fellows worked in other....

Some hospitals...animals were badly wounded. One was killed and we were told that would be our dinner next day.

1945—HUNGER

4TH INFANTRY DIVISION AFTER ACTION REPORT: 5 MARCH 1945 TO D+273—CT 8 advanced against light resistance. In opposing CT 22, the enemy presented a more formidable defense as strong delaying forces fought from key terrain features. In this sector, the enemy made liberal use of mines, booby traps and abatis. CT 12 proceeded against stubborn resistance to the vicinity of Oos. Although fighting a determined delaying action at this point, the Germans were forced to withdraw to the east bank of the Oos River from where they defended fanatically. CT 8 resumed the attack at 0700 with the 2nd Battalion. The only resistance encountered was enemy mine fields. By 0930 the battalion had successfully negotiated four mine fields and had encountered two more while elements of the 3rd Battalion on the left flank continued their advance toward limited regimental objectives. CT 12 resumed the attack with its 1st Battalion at 0700 while the 2nd Battalion was relieved by elements of the 90th Infantry Division. Then the 2nd Battalion assembled in regimental reserve in the town of Büdesheim. Company C advanced to assault the town of Oos and met more opposition than anticipated, so the remainder of the 1st Battalion had to be employed and by 1725, the village was cleared from enemy. The 3rd Battalion initiated an advance and then secured the high ground from which it sent patrols in the direction of Müllenborn. Upon Division order, the 1st Battalion continued its advance from Oos to secure a crossing of the Oos River. At the close of the period, this operation was in process with a firefight near the stream. CT 22 attacked at 0700 with the 2nd and 3rd Battalions to clear the enemy from the town of Duppach. At 1135, Company L had cleared the town while Companies K and I continued the attack to secure the high ground north and east. The attack of the 2nd Battalion proceeded with less speed and Companies F and E repulsed an enemy counterattack. The engagement continued throughout the later hours of the afternoon. By 1900, the situation was clarified and positions were consolidated for the night.

FROM THE DIARY—Monday March 5. Bouillon for breakfast no bread. D— soup with chunks of fat horsemeat. Most fellows couldn't eat it. Same for supper. Complained to captain and got bread. Shortage due to Transport difficulties.

Went to Plaidt on a coal detail. Shoveled briketts (sic) into wagon from Freight Car. They unloaded wagon in a horse hospital.

1945—MOVING TO ANOTHER CAMP

4TH INFANTRY DIVISION AFTER ACTION REPORT: 6 MARCH 1945 TO D+274—Small delaying forces were encountered by our forces at road junctions and towns. At 1340, CT 12 received small arms fire from the vicinity of Müllenborn. The 4th Infantry Division continued the attack, coordinating its movement with the 11th Armored Division. The 8th Infantry assembled as division reserve in prearranged areas at 0920. The remainder of the period was used for rehabilitation of all troops and future plans were formulated for operating as a motorized task force as ordered by the Commanding General of the Division. CT 12 continued the attack to the northeast. During the morning, the 1st Battalion captured the town of Roth and continued the advance to the northeast to affect a crossing of the Kyll river in the vicinity of Nieder Bettingen. The 2nd Battalion moved from its assembly area to the town of Roth and at the close of the period was also advancing to Nieder Bettingen to cross the Kyll river and coordinate a relief of the armored infantry of the 11th

Armored Division. The 3rd Battalion moved also and at the close of the period, was reported to be along the river. Very little enemy opposition was encountered during the day as the movements were behind the 11th Armored Division. The 1st Battalion of the 22nd Infantry was in regimental reserve in the town of Kellenborn while the 2nd Battalion was pushing to the northeast to exploit the bridgehead established by the 11th Armored Division. The 3rd Battalion moved to the town of Ober Bettingen and at the close of the period was preparing to cross the river.

FROM THE DIARY—Tues Mar 6—Went on Bunker detail for the Major's family. Quite hard work digging out gravel from a gravel pit. This was then lined with cement bricks by a regular bricklayer. Here we got apples, cottage cheese sandwich and a bacon sandwich.

Hoped to return next day.

U.K. means unabkömmlich i.e., deferred

4TH INFANTRY DIVISION AFTER ACTION REPORT: 7 MARCH 1945 TO D+275—There were no enemy lines established during the period. Our troops were opposed by rear guard elements. A determined resistance was put up by the enemy along the east bank of the Kyll river and it was not until late in the period that our troops were able to dislodge the opposition from these positions. CT 12, in advancing on Nieder Bettingen and Bewingen, received heavy mortar, machine gun and small arms fire from across the river. The intensity of this fire prevented our troops from effecting a crossing until about 1700. CT 12 met resistance in the form of small forces employing numerous automatic weapons and small arms fire with an infrequent round of artillery. Combat Command B of the 11th Armored Division, after operating within the 4th Infantry Division's zone, was ordered and withdrew to the south to continue the advance through the 90th Infantry Division sector. The 4th Infantry Division captured the towns of Dohn, Bolsdorf, Bewingen and Killescheid. Progress was impeded by lack of adequate bridging facilities across the Kyll river. At the close of the period, Task Force Rhino consisting of the 8th Infantry Regiment and other elements of the Division was preparing to launch their attack early 8 March. The 2nd Battalion of the 12th Infantry crossed the Kyll river in the vicinity of Nieder Bettingen during the night 6-7 March, relieving the armored infantry. During the day, the 2nd Battalion continued the attack and captured the towns of Bolsdorf and Dohn. The 1st Battalion moved rapidly across the river behind the 2nd Battalion. The 3rd Battalion in continuing its advance to cross the Kyll river, cleared the town of Bettingen. After crossing the river, the battalion fought its way to the high ground and occupied the woods. The 3rd Battalion of the 22nd Infantry crossed during the night 6-7 March, the Kyll river in the vicinity of Ober Bettingen and relieved elements of the 11th Armored Division. The battalion received a slight counterattack after completion of the relief but repulsed it quickly. The 1st Battalion and then the 2nd Battalion effected their crossing. During the hours of darkness, 7-8 March, Company E of the 1st Battalion occupied the town of Hillesheim. A treadway bridge was constructed within the 22nd Infantry sector. Throughout the day, Bailey bridge equipment was being brought forward and arrived during the night 7-8 March. Every effort was being made by the 4th Engineer Combat Battalion to complete this bridge by first light of 8 March.

FROM THE DIARY—Wed March 7—awakened at 2:30 AM with curt news, roll your blankets, get ready to leave. We had heard from new arrivals that Wittlich had been shelled by artillery, others said that it was taken. In one hour we were under way—3 men to a loaf of bread and ¼ lb of sausage per man. Destination Limburg. Road was jammed with Army trucks and horse and wagons and the horses for the Horse Hospitals were being evacuated later. What a night for Air Corps if they only knew.

1945—PLACEMENT FOR BATTLE, 100 MEN TO 1 LATRINE BUCKET

FROM THE DIARY—Everything on the other side of Rhine.
3 and 4 trucks pulled by 1.

Red Cross, supply trucks

As we neared Koblenz daylight had appeared and we saw machine gun crews in emplacements as also long trenches on both sides of road.

Koblenz flat as mentioned before, Roads jammed with trucks and horse and wagons.

On shattered buildings in white paint "Koblenz bleibt fest" "Wir halten durch" *(we will persevere)*. People going about the business. Although windows smashed. None in operation.

People more serious than in Miesenheim. Suffering in faces.

Crossed Rhine. Bridge being mined and its approaches. Activity on towers probably MG emplacements.

Over Rhine we walked to Niederlahnstein. Here we were to wait for train until evening of next day. Fortunately we were able to get a boxcar and so we rode to Limburg. 2 KM to PW camp and it was already dusk.

That evening we were quartered in pitch-dark room. Brick floor, no heat, little straw and no supper. One latrine bucket for 100 men. In the morning naturally half was on the floor.

The reality of the prisoner of war experience—the frigid cold of a German winter, the extreme and constant hunger, the never-ending work to be done, the relentless worry of death from sickness or bombings, and the unimaginable filth, unending stench, and health risks resulting from the use of one latrine bucket for 100 starving men, many with dysentery.

1945—ALLIES ADVANCING, SECOND INTERROGATION

4TH INFANTRY DIVISION AFTER ACTION REPORT: 8 MARCH 1945 TO D+276—Our forces advancing rapidly along the entire front met practically no organized resistance. Road blocks, blown bridges, road craters, felled trees and mines constituted the main resistance in the path of the 4th Infantry Division's attacks. While CT 12 and 22 advanced without contacting the enemy, Task Force Rhino swung quickly from across the Kyll river at Ober Bettingen along the northern flank overrunning the enemy to the town of Hoffeld from which point, at the close of the period, armored spearheads were continuing north to the Division's objective at Reifferscheid. The 4th Infantry Division resumed the attack at 0825 when the 8th Infantry, motorized as part of Task Force Rhino under command of Brigadier General Rodwell, initiated the advance. Throughout the day, continuous progress was made against light opposition. The first resistance was encountered at 1305 in the vicinity of Kerpen where a barricade had been erected. This enemy force was eliminated in the short firefight that ensued and the advance continued. Prior to 2200, leading elements were in the vicinity of Honerath, a gain of fourteen miles. The 12th Infantry echeloned forward in its zone of action and established outposts in the town of Zilsdorf and on the high ground to the northwest while the 22nd Infantry readjusted its positions in Hillesheim and on the high ground astride the road immediately to the north.

FROM THE DIARY—Thu Mar 8 So many about 700 GIs were being shipped out that we didn't get any breakfast. Next came interrogation during which my address book was taken (diary in rear) *(This is prohibited via Articles 5 and 6 of the Geneva Convention).*

Then warm soup (well spiced) for dinner and supper. Rumors: Cologne taken

The Red Cross packages which we had awaited so eagerly we would not receive. Part went into our soup e.g., spam, salt and pepper. Remainder doled out every night piecemeal.

At present they were giving out the Canadian Red Cross packages.

On Dec 23 there was an air raid 90 American officers killed. Swiss Red Cross investigated, Britain acknowledged guilt.

Searchlights play on camp now when air raid is on.

That night dreamt that Joe Long was in the Admiralty Islands.

Joe Long was George's best friend from Brewerytown. They grew up together and Joe served as a Marine in WWII. He made it home.

Friday Up at 6:30 AM make bed

Roll call at 7:00—Breakfast 1/6 loaf of bread—Jerry tea

11:30 dinner—soup—smaller quantity than Wittlich but tastier

4:30 PM Roll Call then supper—soup. Then extras—5 cigarettes, 1/3 can of salmon 1 ½ chocolate (Canada) blocks like Hersheys

That day we had Mass said by Chaplain—New Yorker who had Fr O'Brien SJ as instructor at Loyola High. During Mass we had to hit floor several times due to close bombing by our planes. Later we found out that 20 Germans and prisoners (Russian) had been wounded and 1 Russian killed by one of the bombs dropped inside the camp. Some of boys were waiting in a boxcar to ship out. Guards locked doors and went to air raid shelter. Several hurt by shrapnel. 50 cal. Slugs whirring around them.

4TH INFANTRY DIVISION AFTER ACTION REPORT: 10 MARCH 1945 TO D+278—Major General Troy H. Middleton, VIII Corps Commander, presented the Legion of Merit to Brigadier General H.W. Blakeley, Commanding General, at an informal ceremony. The 4th Infantry Division began assembling preparatory to departure from the Third Army sector to the VIII Corps area to the south in the vicinity of Luneville, France.

FROM THE DIARY—Sat Mar 10 one of Jerry guards told me that Altenkirchen had a Stalag which was surrounded by Yanks (Stalag XII D) we are Stalag XII A.

He hoped that we would soon be surrounded. We hear that Koblenz is taken and also Lahnstein both Über and Nieder.

He also said Syria had declared war on Germany. That night we got 2 ½ crackers and actually ¼ lb of butter per man from Canadian Red Cross.

Blühen erweckt in Christian dieselbe zärtliche Liebe, die er als Knabe zu aller Kreatur Gottes gehegt hatte.

So hätte vielleicht das innige Gedeihen ihrer beider Neigung zueinander einen steten Fortgang genommen, hätte Helene nicht die Atmosphäre ihrer häuslichen Umgebung mit sich gebracht, die nun um Christian ein solches Maß von wohlgeordneter und braver Häuslichkeit aufbaut, daß sein zu Extremen geneigtes Temperament, nachdem die ersten Wochen ihrer Vereinigung verrauscht sind, um so heftiger nach einem Ausgleich, einem zügellosen Sichaustoben seines anderen Ichs verlangt.

Vorerst taucht dieses Begehren nur mehr im Unterbewußtsein auf, wird mit Aufbietung aller Kräfte zurückgedämmt und desto ausgiebiger dem geistigen Heißhunger, der sich gleichfalls meldet, Genüge getan. Sein Verlangen, sich über Kunst und Wissenschaft in Briefen auszusprechen, veranlaßt ihn, mit Wieland, dem Dichter von umfassender Bildung, einen Briefwechsel zu beginnen, in dem er ihm seine Ansichten über neue Literatur mit allem Witz und aller seltigen Ironie eröffnet. Durch die Unterdrückung seines geistigen Umganges eigenwilliger im Urteil geworden, stolz in dem Bewußtsein, von einem allseits bewunderten Dichter geschätzt zu werden, sprießen ihm Gedanken und Einfälle bunt und mannigfaltig unter dem Grau des spießbürgerlichen Einerlei seiner Umgebung hervor.

Während er so Wieland gegenüber seinem Unwillen über die literarischen Zustände Luft macht und fühlt, wie seine Kritik sich schärft, sein Ausdruck gewinnt, fällt ihm etwas ein, das ihm tagelang im Kopf spukt und ihn oft so benimmt, daß er nur mit äußerster Anstrengung seinen Amtsverpflichtungen nachkommt.

98

Es müsse doch etwas Köstliches sein, in einem öffentlichen Blatt die gegenwärtige Literatur, Musik, Kunst und Wissenschaft kritisch unter die Lupe zu nehmen, aber auch Enge und Kleinkrämerei, den lähmenden und verlogenen Geist der Philister, mit spritzender, schonungsloser Feder bloßzustellen und zu bespötteln, dagegen die seltenen Taten eines wahrhaft großen menschlichen Herzens zu preisen und so erzieherisch, läuternd und kräftigend auf seine Zeit zu wirken. So könne er anders als auf der Kanzel ein freies, scharfzüngiges Wort wagen, könne weitausholender für sein Vaterland wirken.

Erziehen, du, Christian Schubart, selbst ein Bündel kochender Leidenschaften, noch unruhig hierhin und dorthin fahrend, ohne dich für etwas Ganzes entscheiden zu können? Was berechtigt dich, über ehrbare Bürger zu Gericht zu sitzen, die ihre Pflicht besser tun als du? Vielleicht aber schmölze auch hier alles zusammen, was dich hierhin und dorthin reißt? Und sind die Leidenschaften nicht auch feurige, krafterhaltende Triebe, und hast du nicht ein Recht, den Geist des Alltags, diesen Totengräber des menschlichen Gemütes, zu hassen? Deine Seele verhungert nach Fernsicht, Auftrieb und Höhenluft.

Aber dieser auftauchende Wunsch verflüchtigt sich bald wieder. Vorerst gilt es in den knapp bemessenen Freistunden das Verlangen nach Kenntnissen zu befriedigen. Die Nacht wird zu Hilfe genommen, und wieder wahllos, genießerisch alles durcheinander in sich saugend, arbeitet und liest er, was ihm gefällt, ohne auch jetzt nach dem sicheren Grund zu suchen, auf dem das Gebäude soliden Wissens, die Schulung des Geschmacks sich aufbauen kann. Ist der Kopf bis zum Überlaufen voll Anregung gepumpt, dann wird bei ihm das Bedürfnis nach unmittelbarer Mitteilung und Aussprache im geselligen Kreise bis

99

Syria's declaration of war against Germany and Japan before by March 1945 made it eligible for entry into the United Nations.[87]

4TH INFANTRY DIVISION AFTER ACTION REPORT: 11 TO 14 MARCH 1945, D+279 TO D+282—The 70th Tank Battalion, the 610th Tank Destroyer Battalion and the 377th Antiaircraft Artillery Battalion moved by motor to new assembly areas in the vicinity of Gerbeviller, France. The foot troops of the three regimental combat teams entrained at Bleialf, Germany and detrained at Bayon, France where they were shuttled by motor to their respective billets. The final elements were the foot troops of the 8th Infantry which detrained at Bayon at 1627 on 14 March. All battalions of the 4th Division Artillery left positions in the vicinity of Schwirzheim, Germany, on 11 March between 0900 and 1300. After an uneventful motor march except for 508 flat tires, the 4th Division Artillery closed in the bivouac areas along

Highway 7 in the vicinity of Mersch, Luxembourg, at 2145. The following day all units resumed the march, closing into assembly areas in the vicinity of Puttelange, France, at 1745. Attached to XXI Corps Artillery with the mission of reinforcing the fire of the 63rd Division Artillery, reconnaissance was made during the daylight on 13 March and positions occupied during darkness of 13-14 March. All the battalions fired a preparation at 0300 March 15 and continued firing normal harassing fire until approximately 1600 March 19. The 4th Division Artillery fired 456 missions, expending 2764 rounds of 155 mm and 5850 rounds of 105 mm ammunition. At 1200 March 19, the 4th Division Artillery was ordered to rejoin the 4th Infantry Division. They moved by motor, beginning at 1815, and closed into assembly areas in the vicinity of Gerbeviller at 0430 March 20. Editor's Note: This marked the first time in 199 days (just before the liberation of Paris on August 25, 1944) that the 4ID had not been on the front lines in direct contact with the Germans. Except for a few days, the 4ID was constantly on the front lines and in contact with the German forces from D-Day, June 6, 1944 through VE Day, May 8, 1945. And they'll resume their drive through Germany in a few days after this short break.

FROM THE DIARY—Sunday March 11—Hot (powdered) Milk (sweetened)

Mass and Communion and for extras cottage cheese, raw hamburg meat 2 ½ wheat and meat crackers, 5 cigarettes

1945 RUMORS—TRADING FOR FOOD, FEAR OF TYPHUS

FROM THE DIARY—Monday March 12 Jerry Tea at 7:00

Most of us used it for cleaning messkits since all water is polluted. Also no electricity since last bombing. Today we received double portion of soup at 3:00 PM and that was all for today.

At night we received ½ small box of raisins.

We are forbidden to trade with Russians who usually have bread for sweaters, rings etc. Reason—Typhus

One of trades with Heinies a class ring—2 loaves of bread, sometimes 1 ½ only Loaf of bread also requires 1000 francs or $100.00

Fountain pens, etc. also bring bread. Watches also but they are few and far between. Many taken away on front lines by captors.

Fortunately I was able to get an extra ration of bread for 4 cigarettes.

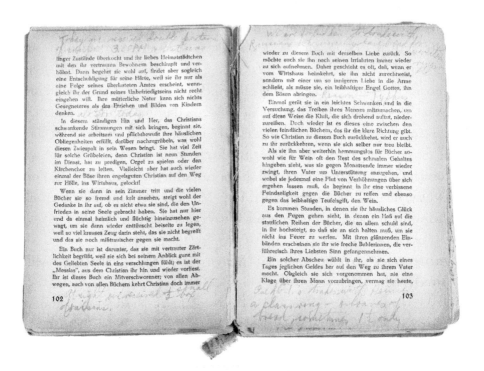

Typhus was carried by lice and the frequent mentions of "delousing" in the diary indicate the prisoners were infested and took care to occasionally rid themselves of the insects. In addition to air strikes, hunger and the close proximity of human refuse, the potential of lice carrying typhus was yet another challenge for the prisoners to address.

Hunger abounded, and trade for food was constant.

Half our time devoted to descriptions of food, other half to killing lice. Everyone is lousy. At night artillery can be heard faintly.

The way George explained it, one of the soldiers would begin by describing the best meal he ever had, in minute detail. Another prisoner might disagree and proceed to explain the "really" best meal, and on it went. The continuous torture of lice biting the flesh, stomachs rebelling from unremitting hunger, the discomfort of frigid winds, and unrelenting sounds of artillery shelling, paint a vivid background upon which the prisoner's daily lives were etched. And the battle lines were drawing closer.

News drifting in, rather rumors says that tank spearhead 10 miles from here. Also Frankfurt is being attacked. Russia declared war on Japan. We are surrounded.

Nazis moving potatoes out by truckloads.

Patton asked Germans to give up. Heard about Gerolstein a labor camp 60 KM NW of Wittlich. 1000 men often 1500 in unheated factory. 8 men to loaf of bread in morning, small ration of thin soup at night. Many sick and undernourished. One man killed by shrapnel while on detail, left under steps for 3 days before buried. One man killed on top floor in strafing Jabo *(fighter bomber)*.

Supposedly investigated by Red Cross.

Supposed to be 6 men to loaf

GI non-coms had knocked down. Other labor camps such as Insch much better off—25 to 75 men. Treated by townfolk. One stole potatoes and eggs from house. Hospitality ceased until GIs beat him up so that he had to visit hospital. Hospitality resumed. One farmer donated a horse to them.

Some claim that the GIs signed a petition and that Jerry Sergeant handed it to Red Cross. Bread supposedly found in GI Sergeant's room.

1945—INCREASING KNOWLEDGE, PREPARING THROUGH CONFESSION, HOLY MASS

FROM THE DIARY—Tues Mar 13—Hot milk
Read "Models for Writing Prose" R. S. Loomis (1931)
Old Savage in New Civilization, Raymond B. Fosdick (1928)
Prometheus Enchained, Stuart Chase—Tech. Review Nov 193?

These refer to English books found in the rubble when the POWs were offsite working. Though the men may have brought them back to use as toilet paper, George took the opportunity to read them.

2PM Tues "All Pvts and PTCs pick up and leave" is order. Just went to Confession.

152

Went out to assembly place where we line up for Roll call twice daily, behind latrine.

Much air activity both Heine and ours. Much bombing and strafing and diving in distance. As names were called off two silver Jabos *(fighter bombers)* whined down on nearby RR yards dropped a bomb. We all hit ground as we watched them execute their graceful dives. Black clouds of smoke and 2 resounding reports.

This broke up the assembly we had to go back to barracks. Here we fortunately heard Mass.

Received communion.

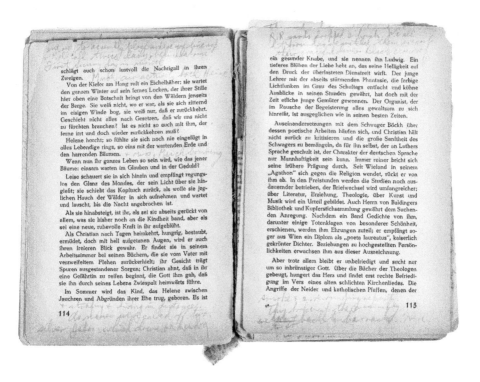

1945—NO MORE BORDERS, HEAVY ARTILLERY,
PRISONERS PHILOSOPHICAL

FROM THE DIARY—Went out later but was not on shipping list.

These bombings hold up Chow for Chow detail cannot fetch same during overhead alert.

Strangely enough <u>after</u> bombs dropped, sirens screamed overhead alert.

Insert—Finished "Lukas Haim" by Tinhofer in wee hours of morning before we left. Religious book moralizing on intellectual pride of hero who realizes his errors after becoming blind.

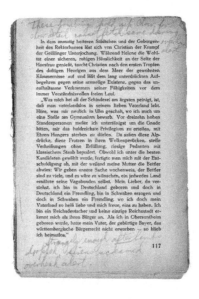

Also in train from Niederlahnstein to Limburg I met a Waldensian descendant. He gave me many interesting facts about Vaudois (settled in Valdese NC) and their language, which is more French than Italian.

Cf. notes on rear of Class Fallotment Cf. History of Waldensians (bet 1937 and 1943) by Prof from Duke UNIV

Waldenses are members of a Christian movement that originated

*in 12th century France. The members followed Christ in poverty
and simplicity. The Waldenses rejected some of the Roman Catholic
beliefs, including some of the sacraments and the idea of purgatory.
They confessed regularly, celebrated communion annually, fasted and
practiced poverty. They rejected prayers for the dead and sainthood and
did not recognize secular courts.[88] A group of Waldenses from Northern
Italy settled in Valdese, North Carolina (NC) in May 1893. They were
pre-Reformation Christians who were persecuted by armies from both
the governments of Italy and France and the official church.[89]*

Jabos *(fighter bombers)* came again later in afternoon and set something
afire in vicinity of RR on airport. When we went out for Roll Call dense
clouds of black smoke rose solemnly above the ruin. Continuing for
hours.

No soup since we had Roll Call 6:15 and gates close at 6:00. So all we
had today was soup once.

We were given ¼ lb of cheese to 3 men and 3 small sardines but
couldn't divide up sardines because it got too dark. Stomach very empty.

10 American cigarettes traded by one fellow for $6.

*To provide context to this amount, $6 in 1945 is estimated to be valued
at $79.15 in 2015. This includes annual inflation of 3.75% for total
inflation of 1,219.17%.[90]*

*The phrase "couldn't divide up sardines because it got too dark" is
striking. The image of grown men huddled in a dark room over three
small sardines on a wood floor trying to figure out how to divide them
equally among the men must have been maddening.*

Wed Mar 14 Got soup for breakfast that we missed last night. It was
sour!

At first some gave it away for cigarettes. Later they gave it away for
nothing.

The Jabos *(fighter bombers)* hit a munitions car and an oil tanker in addition to a building by the railroad yesterday. A guard told me that the bombing last week thus far had caused 8 French deaths and 1 German. In the afternoon fog lifted and we had the sunniest day thus far. Everyone came out and engaged in delousing. The sky was clear and we watched formations of heavy bombers, possibly 500 drone over us. Toward evening Jabos *(fighter bombers)* attacked Railway again. We all watched the diving and the ack-ack *(antiaircraft fire)*. Very few bother about going in-doors.

Read "The Geography Behind History" by Gordon East. Thomas Nelson and Sons Ltd 1942

Interesting to see how the Neolithic culture followed the withdrawal of glaciers in Europe and Asia which moved high-pressure area toward Arctic and diverted Atlantic rains from Steppes (Afrasian desert)

George's interest in history, biography, how things work, why things happened, is being fed.

Lack of rain caused arid deserts followed by departure of man to more fertile spot i.e., valley of Nile, Indus, Tigris and Euphrates. This was followed by development of pasturing, agriculture, weaving, formation of towns and later of cities.

Thurs—Learnt of poor state of German hospitals due to lack of supply. One of medics at Manderscheid mentioned that wounds were covered with single gauze and bandage—the rest was paper. Bandages kept on 4 to 5 days until odor was very fetid. Patients slept on straw beds and usually were all loused up despite efforts of nurses and lay women to keep them clean.

Operations frequent, death rate high, ether as anesthetic; minor operations often performed without. One medic recalls having seen a patient anesthetized with butt of pistol when he became too active for a few men to hold. No face masks little sterility (old school house). Doctors and nurses very capable, lack of medicaments too much.

Have had diarrhea since sour soup for breakfast. Little appetite. Abdomen rigid. Much gas.

1945 NO WAY OUT—MORE INTERROGATIONS

4TH INFANTRY DIVISION AFTER ACTION REPORT: 16-19 MARCH 1945 TO D+284 TO 287—Report G 3 (operations branch): An extensive training program was conducted during four days. This period afforded an excellent chance for rehabilitation for all personnel and for maintenance of weapons and equipment. Full advantage was taken during the time available.

FROM THE DIARY—Fri Mar 16—Went to Diez this morning for questioning. On walls in white paint "Sieg oder Tod" In Volkssturm die Antwort der deutschen Nation. (*"Victory or death"—The Volkssturm refers to the national militia or local Germans between the ages of 13 to 60 years old, who had not been drafted –a last ditch effort to defend Germany)*

FROM THE DIARY—Taken to castle where I was interrogated. Of 20 men I was made to remain in the castle. Placed in single cell with straw mattress and night bowl all to myself #32.

These few simple lines belie the complex content.

It is not clear in which castle he was interrogated, but it could have been the medieval Castle of Diez, which was used as a jail for a period of time up until 1927. There would have been "cells" ready for prisoners, and he notes #32, which might have been his cell number.

The mental anguish of being taken away as a group of 20 men for further interrogation is apparent. Then he watched as the rest of the prisoners returned to the prison camp, leaving him alone in a cell. This provided him with ample time to contemplate. This act was obviously intended to discourage, terrify, weaken, and worry.

Sun came out again yesterday and to accompany our delousing we had music. Bull fiddle guitar sax and piano accordion, competently handled.

"Stardust" brought back many pleasant memories, as also Beer Barrel Polka, Pennsylvania Polka, and Rose of San Antone.

Splendid view looking out over the town from my small window, about 12 stories above ground.

Children playing in the serpentine street, sounds of laughter, horse hooves present a delightful panorama of peace and serenity. This is often interrupted by wail of Air Raid sirens.

Situated close to me in the tower. Interrogated by German Colonel who offered me cigs and whiskey. Became quite angry that I professed to be American and not German. Inquired why German and Americans supported the world but that was prevented by England and US which controlled world market and used Gold which Germany did not have. Germany was interested in a United Europe. He also pointed out that National Socialism or…

Jewish advised President

1945—CONTINUED INTERROGATIONS AND FEAR, YET BEING IN THE MOMENT

FROM THE DIARY—Informed me that my Aunt's neighborhood in Munich had been flattened. She is most likely dead. Interrogator explained that Germany's wish was to trade with…

Communism or Christianity could give a peaceful world only after one of them had conquered. In other words, conquest is a prerequisite before peaceful regime can exist. Efficacy of prayer evidently considered nil.

When the previous arguments failed, the Colonel tried an emotional context.

Colonel pointed out the character of Stalin and ruthlessness of Bolsheviks who slaughtered the German population. How, he said, could US form an alliance with such a nation? Lady Astor's visit to Stalin was also described in which she asked him when he would stop killing and he replied when he had had enough. Lindbergh English home etc. where he had to flee to escape gangster who kidnapped his child was more pro-German than most German Americans. He said I should be ashamed to come over to kill my people. Despite his bitter attitude he returned my salute at end of audience.

Couldn't eat soup brought for supper—still can't belch—gas in stomach. Thought of home. Passed a woman —— something—

Castle this morning who looked like my mother (dressed in black). Went to sleep. Awakened by an air alert.

Was called out for an interview with an Air Corps Officer who spoke excellent English and a friend also in Air Corps.

4TH INFANTRY DIVISION AFTER ACTION REPORT: 17 MARCH 1945, D+285 TO REPORT FROM G-1 (PERSONNEL BRANCH)—The Commanding General approved a division quota of twenty-five officers and 200 enlisted men to visit rest centers at Grenoble (officers) and Lyon (EM) for 5 days.

FROM THE DIARY—Sat Mar 17 St. Patrick's Day, as light began to diffuse into my cell I was already awakened by crowing of cocks and twittering of some birds beneath my window; after given opportunity to work and bread and butter and Jerry Coffee

Music drifted in from Chapel next door. They asked my opinion of the bombed out towns e.g., Koblenz. They pointed out that Germans were much more careful. One of them assured me on his word, as Soldier and Officer, that before they set out for a target, e.g., London, on being briefed their commander would describe the curve in the Thames and the Victoria docks.

Dresden, partial view of the destroyed city center on the Elbe to the
new town. In the center of Neumarkt and the ruins of the Frauenkirche

We went to a room of the castle which belonged to Duke of Nassau.
Many portraits on wall. Strains of organ

Then he promised them punishment if they hit alongside the docks in
the town. In many cases they deliberately let their bombs hit the waterside
rather than strike a town. He said that German night raids were usually
carried out during full moon. British bomb during absence of moon,
hitting indiscriminately. On mentioning Coventry, my questioner
answered me from personal knowledge.

*The German Luftwaffe bombed Coventry, England in November
1940. During "Operation Moonlight Sonata" over 400 bombers
attacked it as it was an important engineering and manufacturing
city. The Luftwaffe selected a night that was bright due to the full
moon. The objective was to desolate the area and sink the morale of the
country. The shock attack was successful. Coventry was poorly defended.
Not one German bomber was shot down despite the number of anti-*

aircraft rounds fired. At the end of the attack, 75% of all buildings were destroyed. The raid deeply impacted the country's morale.[91]

These industries are spread through the town so that it was impossible to hit these without hitting the whole town.

He was surprised that I did not know them for he said most British fliers immediately say, "As for Coventry, we all know that it had many military targets."

He asked about attitude in America. I said that they resent the German attitude of Herrenvolk. He said that the loud to-do about Herrenvolk was made by some few small fry who suddenly obtained a little power.

Herrenvolk democracy refers the master race (in the National Socialist mindset, this would be the Aryans) in charge of the government while the other races are generally excluded.

Actually he said that the Germans wanted to educate the Eastern people, etc. He asked what we thought of Russia and when I suggested the German Russian alliance he pointed out that was a non-aggression pact and not an alliance. Russia taking a part of Poland was a violation of that pact as was seizure of Estonia, Latvia and Lithuania. The break with Russia came, he said, when Germany would not guarantee Poland all of the Balkans and Poland which US and Britain have promised.

One of them says that V-2 or one of them can theoretically reach US and practically soon will. What would be effect on peoples' morale, he asked?

German scientists invented a long-range missile in 1942. The V2 ("Vengeance Weapon") was developed under the leadership of Wernher von Braun, a scientist and member of the SS. This missile was unique in that it was almost impossible to intercept. The first launches of the V2 took place in September 1944, and these were fired on Paris and England. Von Braun used slave labor to produce the V-2, where "thousands of rag-clad prisoners from the Dora concentration camp unloaded parts for the gleaming rockets and then returned to underground tunnels to sleep, and be beaten, in conditions of almost unimaginable filth and contagion."[92] Von Braun was said to be aware of the conditions.

In 1944, von Braun's loyalty to the Reich was questioned and he was detained and taken to a Gestapo cell. After the war, the US and the Soviet Union captured not only samples of the rockets, but also the scientists responsible for them.[93]

By the fall of 1945, von Braun and other scientists arrived at Fort Bliss in Texas. Some went from there to New Mexico. Von Braun continued to develop rockets and missiles for the US, including the Saturn V rocket. Born a Lutheran, he became an Evangelical then later converted to the Episcopalian faith.[94] He died in 1977 and is buried in Alexandria, Virginia.

They stressed accuracy of their fliers pointing out how many cathedrals had been spared in France, Belgium and that this was appreciated by the population. On being asked why Germany invaded Belgium and Holland he replied because they did not guarantee to defend their frontiers against allies.

As for Norway, British fleet was 2 hours under way already when Germans landed. And what about our North Africa landing? Do our papers point how many thousands of women and children are killed as a result of the raid?

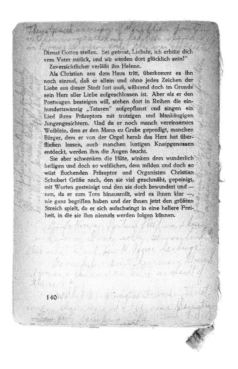

In 1942, the Germans and Italians were in control of a strip of land between Tunisia and Egypt with an army numbering about 100,000 men under the leadership of Rommel. They moved into Tunisia and defeated the Allies, advancing almost 100 miles before being stopped in February 1943. When the counteroffensive failed, the Germans withdrew. The Allies then resumed their offensive under Patton. Within a month, the enemy was cornered. The final attack led to the surrender of about 275,000 Germans and Italians in May, 1943.[95]

Watched kids playing in the winding street, some on skates some on stilts, some playing tag, girls jumping rope.

As I recall one of the officers pointed out that had Germany used ruthless bombing as the English and Americans have, they would have ended the war long ago. This humanitarianism cost them the victory possibly.

One of the officers pointed out that no other people would have been able to withstand such hardships. But the other officer mentioned that that stupid attitude avails them nothing as far as positive results are concerned to which all agreed. One officer, in fact, both believed that US could not hold up under similar trials. Theoretically V waffen can reach US and soon its practical accomplishment will be fact. What will be effect on morale of US people? In my opinion it will only increase the anti-German hatred in the States.

That afternoon left Diez sans Red Cross package. Why I don't know.

He was not able to leave the castle with the Red Cross package, but he was able to leave the castle with his life.

R47s overhead all way, bombing railroad in vicinity of Limburg again. Slept on 3 backjr 2 men 1 blanket.

The war continues. The bombings are getting closer. The front is advancing.

4TH INFANTRY DIVISION AFTER ACTION REPORT: 18 MARCH 1945, D+286—(Nothing reported)

FROM THE DIARY—Sunday March 18, Questioning on Gai Regular Typewritten form. What is a persistent and non-persistent gas Subdivision of gases into tear, coughing, etc.

Means of detection (arm bands, etc.) What would you do if comrade inhaled lung irritant?

(No artificial respiration) How would you treat blister gas on hand? How would you decontaminate a rifle? How often have you been in gas chamber? In US in France? How quickly can you put on your mask? Protective gas mask? Have you ever had it on? Does mask go on first before protective garment? What is DANC? How is gas distributed? Protective Ointment? Mark if you are familiar with M-1, M-2, M-3?

What nerve gases are you familiar with? He had all equipment on table and about 6 or 7 Gas Pamphlets published by US Army.

How many men in Gas Decontamination found?

Met a guard from Cologne who spoke pretty good English although not US or English

Speaking to some PWs who saw Bitburg after it had fallen. Many English slogans on wall.

"See the Rhine and leave your bones there."

US Army vehicles crossing the river Prüm at Lünebach, county of Bitburg-Prümm Rhineland-Palatinate, Germany March 1945

25 miles in 4 weeks—how many dead? 300 miles to Berlin.

Overheard an officer say that the present situation reminded (him) of the film "The Last Days of Pompeii."

Monmartin, seinem Herrn ähnlich mit dem Zug verruchter Niedertracht im Gesicht, der Meister aller dunklen Machenschaften, der jederzeit bereit ist, mit allen Mitteln Geld zu schaffen.

Um so wohltuender fällt Christian inmitten der geschmeidigen Doppelzüngigkeit der Hofleute das gerade und klug blickende Auge des Grafen von Putbus auf, sowie dessen freimütige Worte, die ihm unversehens entfahren, und auch des Grafen stahlblauer Blick sucht oft über die Tafel hinweg den seinen. Ihm ist, als schlüge ihm inmitten des verlogenen Geschmeißes der Fürstenknechte ein aufrichtiges Herz entgegen, und er wundert sich, daß es in dieser Umgebung den kräftigen Schlag behielt.

Mag aber der Organist noch so flüchtig durch das bunt bewegte Ludwigsburg hasten und aus der von schönen Frauen, Virtuosen und Tänzern wimmelnden Oper an seinen Schreibtisch flüchten, sein Geist springt aus der ernsten Hülle und gaukelt schon in unerlaubte Regionen hinüber, zwar nicht auffällig, aber doch wahrnehmbar für feindlich spähende Augen. Einer geheimen Sehnsucht folgend, beginnt er am Sonntag in der Kirche dem rauschenden Allabreve am Schluß des Gottesdienstes hier und da ein Schnörkelchen weltlicher Fröhlichkeit im Stil eleganter Hofmusik einzuflechten und die edlen, einfältig schlichten Linien eines Kirchenstückes in ein barockes Prunkstück zu verwandeln. Wohl ist er sich hierbei einer schweren Verfehlung gegen die Lehren seines Agrell vom Orgelvortrag und Fugenstil bewußt, doch tut es dem eitlen Herzen gar zu wohl, wenn er manchen Kirchgänger, den der Dekan Zilling mit seinen Predigten hinauslangweilte oder mit seinem selbstgefälligen Eifern hinausärgerte, bei Beginn des Orgelspieles wieder in das Gotteshaus zurücklockt.

146

Part 3: Going Home

1945—SINGING, WORKING, ALLIES ADVANCING

FROM THE DIARY—Sang songs in evening Girl of my Dreams and English sang Rose of Tralee, Danny Boy singing others.

4TH INFANTRY DIVISION AFTER ACTION REPORT: 19 MARCH 1945, D+287, REPORT G 1 (PERSONNEL BRANCH)—The 22nd Infantry Regiment was awarded the Presidential Unit Citation and the first badge was pinned on Lieutenant Colonel John F. Ruggles.

FROM THE DIARY—Mon March 19, St Joseph's Day
Many planes overhead. One of them spelt out US with vapor trail.

Though he had a night bowl all to himself in the castle during the interrogations, the familiarity of being back with the other prisoners and singing with them in the deep dark nights without any electricity may have been comforting. One can imagine the notes of familiar songs undulating from one end of the room to the other, bringing with it a blanket of camaraderie and cautious anticipation of life outside of the prison walls.

Saint Joseph's Day held special meaning to George. A day celebrated at his high school and college. St Joseph was the patron saint of workers and the protector of the Catholic Church. Interesting that on this day he sees the planes flying overhead, dramatically spelling out the letters "US" in a vapor trail!

This demonstration of sheer power in the sky must have been an impressive scene, not only to the POWs but also to the German soldiers, to the Germans living in the area, and to the children playing in the streets.

It's over.
We are here.

FROM THE DIARY—Rumor is that 4th and 6th armored Divisions have us cut off. Another rumor is that German Army has taken over government and is asking for peace terms. All Privates and PFCs were to be shipped out tonight except 4 army which was yours truly. 5 men to a Red Cross and as usual I missed it again.

We sleep in triple tier bunks 2 men to a bunk which consists of 3 slats stretched lengthwise with plenty of space in between slats. 4 Blankets. We put 3 down and 1 over. Bed is so narrow that both men must turn at same time. Limeys sleep on opposite side of room. 3 sick men sleep in middle. They came from Gerolstein and look in bad shape—skin and bones.

Transport came back in. Alleged reason for cancellation—bombed railroad. Possibly due to our supposed enclosure by Armored Division. Just thought of guard who saw some GIs scramble for and eat raw potatoes.

4TH INFANTRY DIVISION AFTER ACTION REPORT: 20 MARCH 1945, D+288—The 4th Infantry Division moved from the vicinity of Gerbeviller to the vicinity of Batzendorf, France, under the control of the VI Corps. Advance elements passed the initial point at 0500 and the entire division closed in the new assembly areas by 2030.

FROM THE DIARY—He sympathized with our dietary needs. "One thought that only Russians lived like that"

Overheard 1 GI describe transport in which he participated in which 13 GIs were killed by strafing.

Tues Mar 20—Sun out but weather still cool. 4th and 6th Armored Divisions supposedly have us cut off.

11PM Transport of preceding night is to leave at 2AM. All are to move to forward barracks. 5 failed to do so which resulted in much confusion and bellowing by the guards. One commented "So this is the Kultur the Americans bring"

4TH INFANTRY DIVISION AFTER ACTION REPORT: 21 MARCH 1945, D+289—Because of the large number of officers and men away at other places of recreation, the Commanding General refused a quota to visit a rest center at Nancy.

22 MARCH 1945, D+290—Lieutenant Colonel Arthur S. Teague (22nd Infantry Regiment) was awarded the DSO (British Decoration).

FROM THE DIARY—Wed Mar 21 nothing new Thurs Mar 22 Working for gas interrogator cleaning up office and making one. The Captain is a German Professor lectured at U of Penn, got degree at McGill and taught at Ontario. Head of a German Teacher's College and German Handel (Trade) School in Berlin. Offered us Bread and jelly for breakfast gute welcome since we haven't had bread for 2 days. All bread is supposed to have gone with last transport.

1000 men supposedly went to Hannover. Got some potatoes which we cooked and mashed with butter and salt. Today I felt full.

Traded Bread ¼ loaf for 5 cigs

FROM THE DIARY—Thurs Mar 22—9PM and we are told that camp is to be evacuated.

Prisoners are moving out of Stalag XIIA. "When the time came to leave Stalag XIIA to a more permanent camp, the majority were sent via rail from Limburg station. Depending on their destination this journey could last anything from a couple of days to a week, due to stoppages caused by the constant threat of opportunistic strikes by British and American fighters. There were several instances of planes strafing a train, which against the rules set out in the Geneva Convention, carried no markings on it to indicate that it carried POWs, and as a result, some men were killed or wounded."[96]

"The cattle trucks that the prisoners were herded into were dismal and dirty. Typically 50 men were packed into each car, and most had to stand throughout the duration of the journey, though in some cases it was possible for men to rest in shifts. During transportation very little was provided in terms of food and water. Sometimes men were issued with a large sandwich before departure which they had to make last for a week, while others received nothing to begin with, but were given a foul brand of cheese along the way. Each car contained only one toilet, usually in the form of a deep tin of one description or another. Due to the nature of the diet at Stalag XIIA, the men often suffered with diarrhea during transportation."[97]

We wait outside in cold until 11:30 PM then we are permitted to return to our bunks until 3AM. Friday morning possibly due to the almost full moon which is quite high.

Finally get to train 50 to a boxcar and about 4AM. At 7AM we passed through tunnels but just as we emerged we were hit by P49s which also dropped some bombs. Fortunately we drove back into tunnel and here we remained in the dark all day.

No bread no water doors locked. Tin can, formerly container—now piss can. Helmet liner with cloth, outserved as shit bucket. When used they were passed from man to man until poured out by man sitting next to small ventilator window. No room to stretch out.

The helmet liner was often used as a latrine. When prisoners were transported in boxcars, they would sit for long periods of time. They used the liners to collect urine and feces. The liner was then handed over to whoever was sitting by the slats in the form of a small window.

That person had to press the excrement through the slats. The window seat was never the preferred location.

Finally at 10PM we got a ¼ loaf of bread per man and small piece of cheese. At first guard offered loaf for 50 cigs later would accept 20, but we voted against same.

1945—THE LAST TRAIN RIDE, SINGING, NOT ALL PRISONERS WOULD SURVIVE

FROM THE DIARY—Pulled out into open after dark where we remain all night. Little sleep, plenty arguments, no water yet.

Sing songs and some good harmony. A Limey sang Rose of Tralee among others Danny Boy, etc. were sung by all. In the tunnel where civilians sought refuge a trumpet was playing "Bell Ami" then played some folk songs that the civilians sang. "Nach der Heimat möcht'e ich wieder" *("I want to go home again")* which brought back many memories of home. Will we ever get home? My Mother's birthday will soon be here and her heart must be heavy if she still lives. Every spare moment I pray for her and our speedy reunion. It is the only source of hope and consolation in this life.

This is one of the few moments when his heart is heavy, when the repercussions of living in dire conditions, the intermittent yet unrelenting threats from the Germans on the ground and from the Allies bombing from the air could no longer be tolerated.

And though the prisoners sang together, they were homesick. Deprivation of sleep, absence of food, the stench of war and the claustrophobia of being locked in a box car in tight quarters finally took its toll.

4TH INFANTRY DIVISION AFTER ACTION REPORT: 21 TO 25 MARCH 1945, D+289 TO 293, REPORT G 3 (OPERATIONS)—The 4th Infantry

Division remained assembled, and until 1240 on 23 March, was kept on an alert status with the CT 12 motorized with trucks furnished by the VI Corps and prepared to move on three hours notice. After release from its alert status, the training program was continued, especially in the firing of individual and crew served weapons. Effective at 1200 on 25 March, the Division passed to operational control of the XXI Corps.

FROM THE DIARY—Sat Mar 24—We are to remain here all day exposed to P47s with no water and no bread promised till evening again. At home I would be buying flour for Mom for tomorrow is Palm Sunday.

> *P47s were heavily used in WWII. These were called Thunderbolts and could carry significant bomb loads.*
>
> *"In the night of March 23-24, Montgomery's attack by 25 divisions was launched across a stretch—30 miles long—of Rhine near Wesel after a stupendous bombardment by more than 3,000 guns and waves of attacks by bombers. Resistance was generally slight; but Montgomery would not sanction a further advance until his bridgeheads were consolidated into a salient 20 miles deep. Then the Canadian 1st Army, on the left, drove ahead through the Netherlands, the British 2nd went northeastward to Lübeck and to Wismar on the Baltic, and the US armies swept forward across Germany, fanning out to reach an arc that stretched from Magdeburg (9th Army) through Leipzig (1st) to the borders of Czechoslovakia (3rd) and of Austria (7th and French 1st)."* [98]

Black widow strafed Flak near our train came close to us

Northrop P-61 green airborne (black widow)

The P-61, or the Black Widow, was the military aircraft designed for night-fighting. These aircraft included a pilot, a gunner and a radar operator.

Red Cross and Palm Sunday Psalm 21 applicable

Psalm 21: A Psalm of David
The King rejoices in your strength, Lord.
How great is his joy in the victories you give!

1945—A MISTAKEN BOXCAR BOMBED BY ALLIES, KILLING POWS ON THE LAST MILE

FROM THE DIARY—Around 11:30 AM P47s zoom around, doors locked—exposed on siding—furthermore ventilators were boarded up previously. At about 100 yards away lay a camouflage train. Soon P47s dived in strafing and bombing. First bomb was a direct hit on the train—ammunitions train. Soon it was a raging inferno. We pushed on doors in between dives but guards took off. Some GIs were outside washing (1 car at a time).

Representation of a "Forty-and-eight" boxcar used to transport American POWs in Germany during World War 2, U.S. Air Force photo, National Museum of the US Air Force

1945—BEGGING FOR FREEDOM, HALTING THE BOMBING

P 47N flying over the Pacific during World War II US Air Force photo

FROM THE DIARY—Finally P47s sighted us and came in on us strafing and weaving as they came in their dive. We all hugged floor hoping they would go away but they came a second time. Finally GIs opened door and let us out. 1200—1300 of us ran out on field which offered no protection.

Finally we hit on plan of making human POW and after what seemed ages the letters were formed. I was in the O. We took off our shirts and bent forward so that our backs were exposed. US was clear formed and with toilet paper another PW.

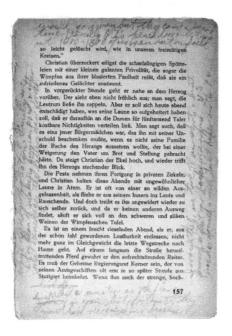

The prisoners were accustomed to bombs falling and sometimes nearer than a hair. The familiar "incoming" calling cards made them brace in fearful anticipation. In reaction, they automatically dove for cover in the boxcar and screamed for their freedom.

In a split second, in a frenzy of quick action, an Allied plane made a direct hit of an ammunitions train too close to the prisoners.

The "BAM" of the thunderous explosives and immense height of

the subsequent and intense fire must have evoked sheer joy to the pilots
above, while wreaking sheer terror on the soldiers below. The end result
was a "raging inferno" 100 yards from George's box car.

The memory of this event was so deeply etched in George's memory
that in 2011, when he was 93, he wrote it out again:

FROM A YELLOW PAD OF PAPER—When American forces approached
Limburg the POW camp was emptied of prisoners and sent eastward.
We were placed in boxcars and were crowded. I and a buddy had lifted
raw potatoes from the kitchen and although we were hungry, we were
afraid to gnaw on the potatoes because the other POWs would have
heard it and would have jumped us for the food.

The trains moved only at night since moving trains were subject to
attack by our planes.

The only toilet facility was a helmet liner into which we urinated and
passed to the man next to the wall of the boxcar which had an open slot
at which the helmet liner was emptied. This caused a lot of dripping and
the men next to it said they would not empty any more.

When we awoke we noticed that a camouflaged train was stationed
on a siding about 100 yards distant from us. This became a target for our
planes. A direct hit set off a series of explosions which showed that the
train contained explosives, which must have made the target even more
appealing for the allied planes.

Then the attacking plane came in our direction and hit one of our
boxcars. We pounded on the doors of the train until the German guards
(in the original diary the Germans left and the US soldiers) opened it. We
evacuated the train quickly, unsure what would happen next.

Someone had the presence of mind to organize a signal to let the plane
know that we were Americans. This was done by having us prisoners
stand in formation on the field adjoining the train so that we spelled out
the letters POW with our bodies. We took off our shirts and stooped
down so that the pilot could see our bare backs and recognize the POW
signal. (I was part of the O). The plane swooped over us amid shouts

from all of us "don't run!" i.e., keep the formation in place. After the plane passed over us it dipped its wings to indicate that the pilot got the message.

We then abandoned the field and continued on foot to the nearest town. There, a physician offered to check all GI's who had medical complaints. I served as interpreter. (Jan 2011)

This account is corroborated by external sources:

"When Allied soldiers began to cross the Rhine in March 1945 the position of Limburg was directly threatened and so the Germans began to evacuate as many prisoners as they could. 1,200 British and American soldiers were packed into the usual railway transport, but the unmarked train was strafed shortly after its departure by US P-47 Thunderbolts and a number of the prisoners were killed. A Scottish padre managed to get some of the men off the train, and in so doing he ended the air strike by ordering them to remove their shirts and arrange their bodies in a field to spell "POW", using the white skin on their backs. The P-47's broke off their attack, but continued to monitor the train in order to ward off other hunting aircraft which may spot the train and regard it as prey. The wounded were moved to a hospital in Limburg, whilst the remainder continued their journey away from the front line."[99]

FROM THE DIARY—What a sensation as the planes dived in again but fortunately they must have recognized us because they didn't strike. We stayed in field all day alternating the letters. Found some raw beets which taste much better than raw potatoes. So we ate beets and deloused awaiting the planes. They came often but only strafed the munitions train which was a regular fireworks. 8 officers and 6 enlisted men were killed and about 40 wounded. Mass was said on field and fitting thanksgiving. Chaplain tried to have ack-acks *(antiaircraft fire)* removed from rear of train and he got permission to have doors opened during daylight if no one took off.

American troops mount a Swedish Bofors 40mm anti-aircraft gun near the Algerian coastline in 1943 Maurice, cap sur le Hoggar, de l'Atakor à la Taessa. Original uploader was Lecarteldz at fr.wikipedia - Library of Congress, Prints & Photographs Division, FSA-OWI Collection, Reproduction number LC-USW33-000888-C DLC. Image source: U.S. Army Signal Corps....
Anti-aircraft bofors gun in at position on a mound overlooking the beach in Algeria with a United States anti-aircraft artillery crew in position.

1945—FREE YET STILL IN CHAINS

FROM THE DIARY—That night moved to another car where there were only 40 men but my head was next to the shit bucket (uncovered). All night used frequently by those who had GI's *(presume this refers to gastrointestinal disorders)*. Strafed by Black Widows twice Flak fired at it. Doors locked again (Eschenhofen). Finally got off. Next morning Palm Sunday after 25 KM came to beautiful section near Kirchenhofen.

US and PW were painted on top of boxcar so we were more confident. Finally got our ¼ loaf of bread.

I still had some raw beets which tasted perfectly. Stream to wash in, heard Mass and singing and enjoyed perfect Sunday

Along winding stream where we washed, shaved and deloused. Perfect Palm Sunday

Palm Sunday—the day Jesus rode into Jerusalem on a donkey. The people celebrated his arrival by laying palms out before him. A donkey symbolizes an animal of peace. They were welcomed as free men.

FROM THE DIARY—Only an occasional Landser (local person) played on trumpet and also phonograph and it seemed like a picnic. We sang Lili Marlene, Beer Barrel Polka.

Lili Marlene was popular with both Germans and the Allied soldiers during WWII. It was initially written as a poem in 1915 during WWI "The Song of a Young Soldier on Watch."

That night (locked up) we all sang "Mother Michele" "Danny Boy" etc.

Competing with us were the Landsers in next wagon "Lilli Marlene" In der Heimat gibt's ein Wiedersehen. Nach der Heimiat möcht'e ich wieder" *(At home there is a reunion, I want to go home again).*

Traded rings for cheese and bread. Black Widows looked us over but no action. Tunnels blown up around us, supposedly keep us here. We reversed static.

4TH INFANTRY DIVISION AFTER ACTION REPORT: 26 TO 27 MARCH 1945, D+294 TO 295, REPORT G 3 (OPERATIONS)—Movement was begun by motor at 0700. The 12th Infantry Regiment with the 42nd Field Artillery Battalion and companies from other units attached, closed into its new assembly area in the vicinity of Ellerstadt, Germany, by 1600.

The 22nd Infantry Regiment with the 44th Field Artillery Battalion and companies from other units attached, moved to the new assembly area in the vicinity of Lambrecht, Germany, closing there by 2100. All other elements of the Division remained in the vicinity of Batzendorf until 27 March when movement of the 8th Infantry Regiment with the 29 Field Artillery Battalion and other companies from other units attached, was completed by 1545 to the vicinity of Bad Dürkheim, Germany. The 70th Tank Battalion and the 610th Tank Destroyer Battalion went into bivouac for the night in the vicinity of Hainfeld, Germany, in order to release road priority for movement of the 12th Armored Division across the Rhine.

FROM THE DIARY—Mon Mar 26 Went to stream and washed.

Cloudy and rainy Deo Gratias *(Praise God)*

We are to leave for a Stalag by walking. All in favor of that. Met a Landser who said it was a shame that US fights Germany when 50% of us were of German descent. In Diez Colonel estimated it 60%

Other day Landser who nailed up windows when asked how long trip will last said "Length of the War" Maybe he is right.

At this point, the prisoners were on their own, but in enemy territory. They were looking for American troops to liberate them. The next few entries describe his experiences walking through the towns, of moving around in groups, of Allied soldiers never sure of what lay around the corner. How odd to think of German and American soldiers just passing by each other and conversing. After all, it's still a time of war.

Mon evening set out on our march. Walked on. Guards drunk. Some GIs drunk from cognac. Many took off. Many painted way to liberty. Some guards even took off with GIs. About 4 groups took off near Weilburg when they heard Yanks were 4km off. They were to tell the Yanks where we were headed. Finally got to Brauenfels. Many Jerrys dug in with bazookas, evidently awaiting tanks. Beautiful castle and many luxurious homes. Stayed in barn. Mother's birthday. News arrives we are surrounded. Are to move about as we wish. We finally get Red Cross packages. Doctor holds office hours for GIs many sick.

1945—WALKING HOME

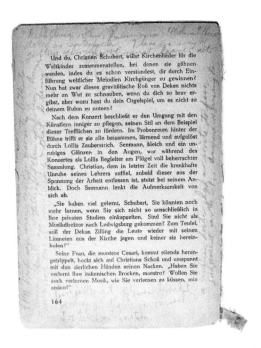

FROM THE DIARY—Diphtheria, Flu, Pneumonia Medical Office. Active as Interpreter. There is a way of getting through we must leave at 8PM. Doctor says many can't go and writes letter to German lieutenant telling of their conditions. Answer comes back that all must leave and that he being a civilian doctor had no right to pass judgment on the GIs. Anyone refusing to leave will be shot. SS men brandishing revolvers get all sick men on road. Doc taken into custody.

When asked later in life about the German doctor being taken into custody by the SS for helping the prisoners, George had no memory of it.

We packed through Wetzlar all deserted.

Machine gun and rifle fire on the other side of the Lahn. No trucks or people on road. Finally reached Dudenhofen where we slept in field later in barn. Sudden shellfire awoke me. There is Jerry Artillery set in back of house. Fire all around us.

Finally a GI tank comes around in a bend in street. We are liberated! 11:00 AM Wed Mar 27. I had to cry.

National Archives: WWII, Europe, Germany, " 1,200 US soldiers escape from POW camp at Limburg, Germany" - NARA—195464

The scene is remarkable not only for the climax of liberation, but also because a resilient man who rarely showed emotional responses was so "moved to tears" that he was finally able to release the energy that held him together during this humbling, complicated and lonely period of his life.

While George and the escapees were liberated on March 27, 1945, he would have been better served staying behind, as Stalag XIIA was liberated two days earlier on March 25, 1945.[100]

Soon we all marched away. Jerry guards nervous but soon reassured by us. Jerry loosely put arms around our boys. He had treated us fine all along. Walked to Atzbach where we were given cigs, candy by 7th Armor.

Colonel as he marched into town. Stayed in schoolhouse overnight on straw. GIs wrecked school. I remember propaganda books and some magazines, race cultures, etc. Glass cases broken chicken looted etc by GIs.

Jelly and preserves taken from cellars bicycles likewise. Wine and cognac also in evidence. Italians gave me wine. Poles glad to return home. Had been forced at pistol point (men and women) to come to Germany.

That night, the prisoners slept in an old school house. George remembered the propaganda books from his time at the University in 1939 and went in search of them. He found a sack and loaded as many books as he could carry. In spite of his weakness from hunger and walking, he managed to carry these heavy books in the large sack all the way back home to Philadelphia.

Jerry's scared. All have white flags put out of window. Had been told that women would be demanded, men castrated and many shot. Gave them some rations for which they were grateful. All thankful that war is over for them even though they have lost husbands and sons. Thursday we march off in direction of Wetzlar.

14 of us separated from column *(formation of soldiers marching together in which the length is longer than the width)* after a lift from a jeep. Had supper with potatoes, peas, meat canned peaches, GI coffee, cream,

sugar, white bread, marmalade. Given candy, cigarettes, soup, etc. Then shipped on and picked up by wire laying group.

Their captain took charge of us and gave us 3 bottles of champagne. Pineapple (crushed) also given us. Not knowing where we belonged they took us with other outfit to Kraftldorf

Here we bedded overnight with Medics. Got 3 fried eggs in morning and raisin bread and prunes.

All outfit moving. Can't catch up with Jerries long enough to fire a shot. Rumor has it 1. War over 2. 3 day lull 3. Jerries will see to it that GIs reach Berlin before Russians if they have to help them themselves

By Ambulance where we will be deloused and given fresh issue of clothes.

Tänzers jene dunkle aus Ekel, Gier und Überdruß erzeugte Unruhe, die ihn schon bei den Festlichkeiten trieb, eine Witze mit einer beißenden Schärfe zu würzen, laut zu lärmen und zu lästern, um nicht die unbequeme Mahnung zu hören, daß er tief, allzu tief in einem Labyrinth gefangen sei, aus dem er schwer und vielleicht nie mehr einen Ausweg finden werde.

Die Ausgelassenheit steigt in hitzigen Wellen und muß in einem nahen Gasthaus bei neuem Champagner gekühlt werden. Als Seemann aufgebrochen, lauert die Cesari dem trunkenen Christian auf, um ihn mit energischen Griffen in einen dunklen Seitenraum zu zerren und ihren heißen Mutwillen bei ihm zu stillen.

Proben und wieder Proben rufen Christian alsbald vom Hause fort in die Oper und geben ihm Gelegenheit, Aufführungen zu hören und mit den Künstlern und den verwöhnten Sängerinnen zu zechen, zu lieben, zu lästern und gesättigt und dennoch voll Unruhe im Strom weltlichen Genusses zu schwimmen.

Die Aufführung der Kantate geht mit großem Erfolg und jubelnden Beifallsbezeugungen der Klostermitglieder vorüber. Jedoch wohnt ihr der Dekan Zilling nicht bei, da, wie er, seine massige Gestalt hoch aufrichtend, dem Regierungsrat Kerner zu verstehen gibt, eine Musik von diesem lockeren Volke aufgeführt Gottes Ohren nicht angenehm sei, auch wenn sie den Menschen lieblich klinge. „Manches flötet gar süß auf Schalmeien und sitzt doch der Teufel dahinter!"

Die übliche Nachfeier folgt, und Christian, an einem Arm die Cesari, am anderen die Bonavini, zieht trällernd ins Wirtshaus, wo er nicht nur die Sterne der Oper, sondern auch Maler, Gartenkünstler, Theatermaschinisten antrifft und es sich in ihrem bunten Kreis wohl sein läßt.

170

1945—CAMP LUCKY STRIKE IN FRANCE, WHERE THOSE WHO MADE IT, MADE IT

FROM THE DIARY—Good Friday finally got to Luftlager near Wetzlar Took plane C-47 at Gießen. Arrived at Le Havre. Candy again, pipes band

Good Friday commemorates the crucifixion of Jesus Christ. It is a somber remembrance of the ultimate sacrifice of life.

And this is where the diary ends. Towards the end of the book on the final pages, he wrote a few ideas he must have had or things he heard while a prisoner.

1. Story of Norwegian soldier
2. Story of Pole who asked to be excused to pray for 1 hour
3. GI of 9th reported dead picture in hometown paper
Vitamins—Regular Diet
At Gulag studied Norwegian

It's a coincidence that #3 describes a GI who was reported dead in his hometown paper. And that is precisely what happened to George. What an interesting foreshadowing of his own life.

1945—WHAT HE DID SO THAT HE WOULD REMEMBER

In addition to these story ideas, you will find a list of Russian chemistry terms at the end of the book. How he came to learn these terms is very interesting, and something he remembered well. There was a Russian guard at the prison camp who defected to the German side. He had a Russian/German dictionary. George asked to borrow it to write down a few chemistry terms, and he set about memorizing them.

At night, when there was nothing to do and light was scarce, he would say the word aloud first in Russian and then in English. He went down the list and continued to practice.

One night, he remembered getting stuck on a Russian term, not remembering what it was in English. He kept repeating it, hoping he would remember, when finally a GI nearby said, "For crying out loud, it's fermentation!"

1945—WHAT HE BROUGHT BACK SO THAT WE WOULD REMEMBER

Earlier in the diary, George wrote about the night he spent in the school in Wetzlar and the time he took to locate some of the propaganda books that they used to teach. While it's not the typical war treasure, he saw these as important historical artifacts, documents to remember the intent to misinform, and in this case, to misinform youth. He remembered the difficulty carrying the sack of books with him, as he was weak, tired, hungry, and very thin at this point. He was helped by a fellow GI who remarked, "These must be really valuable for you to be carrying such a heavy load."

The books are quite unsettling and a reminder of the evil power of hatred. And though the practices of using Nazi propaganda to teach prejudice are well documented, it's difficult to fully comprehend until you actually see the material they used.

One of the books is an over-sized book for children entitled "Erblehre, Abstammungs—und Rassenkunde in Bildlicher Darstellung" (Heredity, Geneology, and Racial Science in Pictures) by Alfred Vogel. It's essentially a picture book that was used in schools, presumably to indoctrinate children. It starts with the concept of pollination and shows how when plants cross-pollinate they lose their roots and become a blend of different plants.

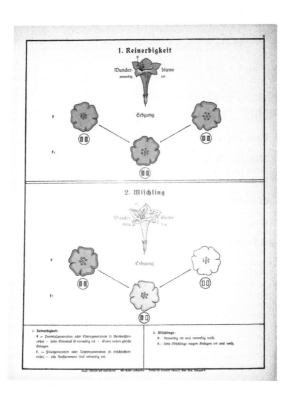

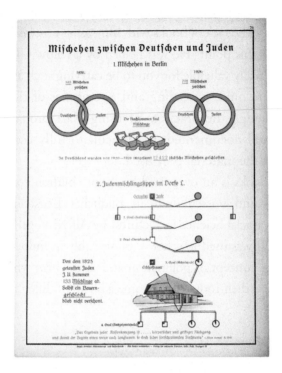

It expands this concept and aims to teach children the negative effects of mixing blood lines, and the importance of keeping the race pure. This picture depicts the impact of German—Jewish marriages and how these will essentially mix races and destroy racial purity.

He also brought home "Schriften zu Deutschlands Erneuerung" (Writings on Germany's Renewal), which is a set of 12 books that cover Germany's history, including the Third Reich, the importance of keeping the race pure, and geopolitics.

There was also a paperback by Herbert Ludat on Poland, and a very fragile magazine-type book focused on Adolf Hitler.

In addition to these, he had a number of swastika armbands that he may have brought back from his time in 1939 or from his return trip in 1944-1945.

4TH INFANTRY DIVISION CASUALTIES FOR THE MONTH OF MARCH 1945

KILLED IN ACTION: 9 officers, 174 enlisted
MISSING IN ACTION: 0 officers, 8 enlisted
SERIOUSLY WOUNDED IN ACTION: 3 officers, 69 enlisted
LIGHTLY WOUNDED IN ACTION: 29 officers, 480 enlisted

TOTAL CASUALTIES: 41 officers, 731 enlisted

7. From Camp Lucky Strike to The Manhattan Project

THE POWS FROM LIMBURG WERE SENT TO A CAMP IN FRANCE BEFORE RE-turning Stateside.

Signal Corps photo dated May 25, 1945

George was sent to Camp Lucky Strike, which was a "cigarette camp" so named to disguise its geographical location. It was primarily used to house repatriated soldiers and liberated POWs from Germany, and also as a station for soldiers on leave.[101]

And as soon as George made it to France, he picked up a French/English dictionary.

Life at the Camp had its challenges, but by 1945, it offered permanent structures, including a mess hall.[102] It was split into four areas, each composed of 2,900 tents, which housed an estimated 14,500 men.

From Lucky Strike, he returned home to Philadelphia. No one knew how close he came to death many times, even on the last mile in a boxcar when 14 fellow prisoners met their end.

George was quite thin at this point, and his teeth were in very poor shape. But he was still enlisted.

FROM A YELLOW PAD OF PAPER—On returning to Philadelphia (after the POW experience), I made the discovery that my mother had received a telegram from the army stating that I had been killed in action. My picture even appeared on the first page of the Philadelphia Inquirer in February 1945.

The Pastor (from St. Ludwig's) took my mother to the Red Cross to learn how she would receive my insurance. There she was told that it was not I who was killed in action, but her other son. Since she had no other son she decided that the announcement of my death was an error.

Later she received a telegram from the army that confirmed her suspicion. It stated that I was missing in action.

Soldier Reported Dead Is Missing

Private First Class George J. Beichl, 26, former professor of chemistry at St. Joseph's College, who last week was reported killed in action in Germany, should now be considered as missing, according to a War Department telegram received yesterday by his mother, Mrs. Louisa Beichl, of 1430 N. Dover st. No details were given in the latest notification.

A member of the college faculty since 1939, Private Beichl entered the Army last Aug. 9. He went overseas last month.

One evening I visited Meschler's tavern over on the SE corner of 29th and Girard with a group of friends. As we were sitting there I noticed one of the fellows who frequented the Fairmount Liedertafel eye me as he circled the table. He bent down to the fellow next to me and asked him in a voice loud enough to be heard by all, "Iss dot Chorch Beichl?" When he was assured that I was he, he came over and embraced me and said "I tought you was dead." Franzl came from Kärnten (Carinthia) in Austria.

I also took the opportunity to visit friends at St. Joe's College and the University of Pennsylvania.

"When I saw (George) in the summer of 1945 he was emaciated and I guess he hardly weighed 100 pounds for a man six feet tall. Only after he almost lost his life, the military finally realized George was a first class chemist and mathematician. So he was reassigned to the then secret Atom Bomb project at Los Alamos in New Mexico."[103]

At the University (of Pennsylvania), the Chairman of the Chemistry Department, Dr. Hiram Lukens (he was a descendant of one of the 13 families who came from Krefeld in 1683 to establish the first German settlement in America, Germantown, which was incorporated into Philadelphia) asked me what I was doing in the infantry since I had an MS in Chemistry. I told him that that wasn't my idea.

Dr. Lukens said, "We will get you assigned to the Manhattan Project. See Professor Ralph Connor" (Organic Chemistry) who subsequently became a Vice President at Rohm and Haas. He had been doing work with RDX, an explosive used in the fabrication of the bomb. I gave him my serial number and he promised to have me reassigned to the Manhattan Project.

And he was ordered to go to Atlantic City for a few days R&R (rest and relaxation).

After a week at home I had to report for two weeks of R&R (rest and relaxation) at Atlantic City, specifically at the Hotel Dennis. I went with Hughie O'Brien from Trenton, a PW whom I had met at Camp Lucky Strike in France.

Hughie enjoyed visiting the tap rooms in Atlantic City and could not be convinced that he should return to his lodgings since the following morning we were to have our physical examinations.

Early the next morning we had to report for inspection in the corridor of the Hotel Dennis. Everyone showed up except Hughie O'Brien. On being asked who his roommate was, I responded and said that Hughie was sick.

The sergeant did not buy this excuse and went to our room with another soldier. On failing to arouse Hughie from his deep sleep with several vigorous shakings, he asked the soldier with him to bring him a pitcher of water. As soon as this was made available he drenched poor Hughie who had failed to disrobe before falling asleep.

This had the desired effect and Hughie woke up flailing his arms, shouting all shades of obscenities until he opened his eyes and saw the sergeant hovering over him. He then joined us in the physical and intelligence examinations. These lasted two days, after which we were free to relax on the sand and sea.

Unfortunately I never had a chance to enjoy this. I received an emergency telegram. Report to Oak Ridge, Tennessee, immediately.

And so George made his way to Oak Ridge, Tennessee.

But I was not given an assignment right away. It seems they had difficulty clearing me. My former boss at St. Joseph's College, Father Molloy, later explained how he was interrogated. One man asked questions and the other watched his reactions. One question was "Did you know that Beichl belonged to a German singing club? And that he was with them in New York at a Sängerfest?"

He replied "Yes, he told me about it."

"Did you know that Fritz Kuhn spoke there?"

Father Molloy immediately replied that he had no idea who spoke there.

Fritz Kuhn was the Head of the "German American Bund", which was a Nazi organization. Had the Secret Service been more perceptive, they should have worried that I was a communist sympathizer since I belonged to the Arbeitergesangvereine, which had many socialist and communist ideologies in its central organization. The Liedertafel (the club to which I belonged) was founded by brewers who were strong union supporters. We members of a later generation did not have their political sentiments.

The American Nazi leader, Fritz Kuhn, spoke at important venues, including a speech in February 1939 at Madison Square Garden.

Kuhn, who had a master's degree in chemical engineering from the Technical University of Munich, became a naturalized US citizen in 1934. In 1939 Kuhn was jailed for misappropriation of Bund funds, around the same time that Hitler invaded Poland.[104] *His citizenship was revoked and he was deported in 1945.*[105]

Oak Ridge was the facility at which U235 was separated from U238. The 235 mass isotope of uranium was the species that could be split when neutrons struck it. This was accomplished by diffusion of the volatile UF_6.

A large labor force of civilians carried out this process by turning valves and following the directions given them by the scientists in charge. The U235 became the fissionable component of the bomb dropped on Nagasaki and plutonium was the fuel employed in the attacks on Hiroshima.

V.J. Day, commemorating the victory over Japan was a cause of great celebration. The army newspaper interviewed several of the local residents, inquiring of them what they thought of the role played by the Oak Ridge laboratory in bringing the war in the Pacific to its conclusion. This was moonshine country and still abounded in the hollows. One knowledgeable resident gave this opinion, "This don't surprise me. I always know that this was a powerful country."

V.J. Day had a salutary effect on my assignment to the Manhattan Project. I received (full) clearance.

—George Beichl

Socializing was commonplace for the scientists working on the Manhattan Project.

FROM A YELLOW PAD OF PAPER—In 1945 I was assigned to the Manhattan Project at Los Alamos and was invited to a party in Santa Fe by a fellow GI whose wife lived there. It was in the home of a Swiss fellow and after a while we were singing and I got them to sing some German songs.

One fellow, with a heavy German accent, came to me and asked where I learned those songs. I told him I belonged to a German chorus and in passing, mentioned that it was a member of the Working Men's Singing Societies.

He then asked me "Do you know the song 'Tor Folesson'?"

That is a song about a Swedish worker who fought the capitalist bosses. I told him I knew of the song but we never sang it.

Then, he replied "Then you were not a member of a Working Men's Singing Society."

Tor Folesson was a hero to the socialists. I think he threw a rock into a machine in the factory where he worked.

Which led me to think, what in the world was he doing in such a sensitive area? (Meaning around sensitive information)

I worked at Los Alamos the summer following my discharge from the Army.

On returning to Philadelphia I received a call from the FBI who wanted to meet with me since I was applying for a position at Los Alamos. I told him that I had just completed working there and had no intention of returning.

His reply was "Thank God, I am having a hard time clearing you."

And all of this stemmed from the fact that I had been active in a German Singing Society. It is interesting to note that David Greenglass and the Rosenbergs transferred some important data on the A-bomb from Los Alamos to the Soviet Union and evidently had no difficulty in being assigned there.

—George Beichl

Julius and Ethel Rosenberg were convicted and found guilty of espionage conspiracy and sentenced to death. Julius (a Soviet spy) was said to have passed atomic secrets to the Soviet Union that he received from Ethel's brother David Greenglass. Greenglass was an army sergeant at

Los Alamos (Manhattan Project). Their supposed reasons for stealing the intelligence were rooted in ideology and belief in communism. [106]

George met many other scientists, including Robert Oppenheimer and Klaus Fuchs. Emil Julius Klaus Fuchs was a German-born British theoretical physicist and atomic spy, who in 1950 was convicted of supplying information from the American, British, and Canadian Manhattan Project to the Soviet Union, evidently believing in Communism. Fuchs was responsible for many theoretical calculations related to the first nuclear weapons, and later, early models of the hydrogen bomb. He died in 1988.[107]

George saved a number of photos from his time in Oak Ridge and Los Alamos.

Here's a photo of his Army jacket with both an Infantry patch as well as one from the Manhattan project. It's unusual to see this compilation. How many scientists on the Manhattan Project previously served in the Infantry during the same war and were captured as a POW? And George was proud of both patches.

He was honorably discharged March 22, 1946 from Fort Bliss, Texas and at the time of his departure, his separation payment for the time served domestically and abroad totaled $210.

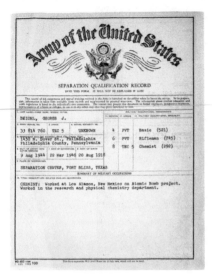
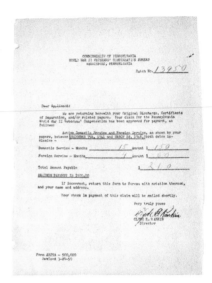

Most importantly, he did not forget the kindness of his prison guard and friend Karl Schäfer and the corresponding risks that the seasoned and injured German Guard and his wife took to help him survive. He was grateful.

Below is a letter found in George's top desk drawer, from Karl in 1946. It seems that George wrote Karl and offered to help him, and this was Karl's response:

TRIER, den 17. Juni 1946

Lieber Georg!

Deinen lieben Brief vom 15. Mai heute
mit Freuden erhalten, Du warst schon als
gefallen in deiner Heimat gemeldet, dest
größer wird die Freude deiner Mutter gewesen
sein, als sie wieder ein Lebenszeichen von
Dir erhielt. Wie es zur Zeit in Deutschland
ist wirst Du unterrichtet sein, Trier ist mit
2/3 zerstört, Baumatrialien gibt es sehr
wenig, da auch die meisten Brücken beim
Rückmarsch gesprengt wurden, und so keine
Verbindung nach den anderen Industrie
Städten herrscht. Den letzten Winter habe
wir mit Not überlebt, jetzt im Sommer
braucht man wenigstens keinen Brand
auch gibtes schon mal Gemüse, es geht
schon etwas besser.
Lb. Georg als Du damals in Wittlich warst-
habe ich Dir gerne geholfen, leider war
es nur für kurze Dauer, dafür verlange
ich heute aber keine Gegenleistung von
Dir, nicht daß Du der Meinung bist, ich
hätte nur aus diesem Grunde geschrieben.
Ich bin zur Zeit wie soviale arm wie eine
Kirchenmaus, meine ganze Wohnung mit
Inhalt total zerstört bezw. verbrannt
zu kaufen bekommt man wenig, höchstens
gegen Tausch. Wenn Du mir etwas schicken
willst, so wäre am besten Rauchwaren
Kaffee, Seifa Tee da sich dieses am besten
verschicken läßt und ich kann andere Sachen
dafür tauschen, auch sind diese Artikel
sehr rar hier.

Trier, den 17 Juni, 1946

Lieber Georg!

Deinen lieben Brief vom 15. Mai heute mit Freuden erhalten. Du warst schon gefallen in Deiner Heimat gemeldet, desto größer wird die Freude deiner Mutter gewesen sein, als sie wieder ein Lebenszeichen von Dir erhielt. Wie es zur Zeit in Deutschland ist wirst Du unterrichtet sein, Trier ist mit 2/3 zerstört. Baumaterialien gibt es sehr wenig, da auch die meisten Brücken beim Rückmarsch gesprengt wurden, und so keine Verbindung nach den anderen Industrie Städten herrscht. Den letzten Winter haben wir mit Not überlebt, jetzt im Sommer braucht man wenigstens keinen Brand, auch gibt es schon etwas Gemüse, es geht schon etwas besser.

Lb. Georg als Du damals in Wittlich warst habe ich Dir gerne geholfen leider war es nur für kurze Dauer, dafür verlange ich heute aber keine Gegenleistung von Dir, nicht dass Du der Meinung bist, ich hätte nur aus diesem Grunde geschrieben. Ich bin zur Zeit wie soviele arm wie eine Kirchenmaus, meine ganze Wohnung mit Inhalt total zerstört bezw. verbrannt, zu kaufen bekommt man wenig, höchstens gegen Tausch. Wenn Du mir etwas schicken willst, so wäre am besten Rauchwaren, Kaffee, Seife, Tee, da sich dieses am besten verschicken läßt und ich kann andere Sachen dafür tauschen, auch sind diese Artikel sehr rar hier.

Wir bekommen pro Kopf alle 4 Wochen 4.40 gramm Fleisch, 6000 gramm Brotfett (Butter) 325 gramm… USw. Zucker kennen wir gar nicht mehr. Kartoffeln 12 Pfd im Monat, jetzt kannst Du dir ein Bild machen. Ich arbeite jetzt als Maurer und bei dieser Arbeit gibt es Hunger, nun habe ich genug Leid geklagt und will daher schliessen.

Herzliche Grüsse auch an Deine Mutter,

Karl Schäfer

Lieber Herr Beichl!

Es freut mich sehr, daß Sie gesund zu Hause angekommen sind. Die Freude Ihrer Frau Mutter kann ich mir gut vorstellen. Wir haben sehr oft von Ihnen gesprochen. Sollten Sie einmal wieder nach Deutschland kommen sind Sie jederzeit herzlich willkommen. Wir haben uns zwei Zimmer zurecht gemacht und geht es uns der Zeit entsprechend. Die Wohnungsnot ist noch sehr groß hier aber die Leute sind sehr bescheiden geworden.

Herzliche Grüße und alles Gute auch für Ihre Frau Mutter,

Gretel Schäfer

Translated:

Trier, 17 June, 1946

Dear George!

I was so glad to receive your letter of 15 May today. Though you were already reported in the US as killed in action, how much greater was your Mother's joy once she realized that you were still alive. I'll have to tell you how it is in Germany these days. Trier has been 2/3 destroyed. There is little in the way of building materials and the bridges were blown up so we have no direct access to other industrialized cities at this time. We made it through a difficult winter, and now in summer it is a little easier as we don't need things like heat, and we grow vegetables, so it is a little bit better.

Dear George, I was very glad to help you out when you were in Wittlich; unfortunately only for a short duration. So I don't want you think that because I helped you that I expect you to help me too, and that's the only reason I am writing you back. Right now I am as poor as a church mouse. My entire apartment was completely destroyed, burnt. One is able to buy very little unless it can be bartered. So if you did want to send something the best things would be: cigarettes, coffee, soap and tea, because they would be easy to send, can be easily traded, and also these items are pretty rare.

Every four weeks we receive per person 4.40 grams of meat, 6000 grams of bread, butterspread *(butter)*, 325 grams…etc. (We don't know what sugar is anymore). 12 pounds of potatoes per month, just to try and paint a picture for you. I work now as a mason and unfortunately this kind of work leaves you hungry. But I have complained enough about our suffering so now I'll close this letter.

Warm regards also to your Mother,
Karl Schäfer

Dear Mr. Beichl,

I'm glad that you made it home healthy. I can imagine the joy your Mother felt when she saw you again. We have often talked about you. Should you ever return to Germany, you are gladly welcome here anytime. We have two rooms we are good considering the time. There is still a great need for living quarters here but the people have become very modest and humble.

Warm regards to you and also to your Mother,
Gretel Schäfer

The physical and emotional effects of the Allied bombings left Germany deeply scarred. Cities and towns were devastated. Communications channels and bridges were severely damaged. The isolation was deafening.

But they were not forgotten.

George's mother was grateful to Karl and his wife for taking so many personal risks to save her son. Though she also did not have much, she had enough to share. And so she began to mail "care packages" with whatever staples she could afford to send. This continued over a period of time until the situation in Germany improved. And it set in motion the continuation of a friendship across the divide.

As the horror of the genocide of the European Jewish community was fully revealed, Germany faced tremendous animosity and scorn. Though the reign of National Socialism had finally ended, the shadow of the atrocities fell over the now divided (East-West) country.

To rebuild Europe and to prevent the spread of communism, the Marshall Plan (Economic Cooperation Act) was passed by the US Congress in March 1948.[108]

And as individual Germans tried to put the pieces back together, they also needed financial aid. Many families in the US with German roots generally tried to help. In fact, a few months after the Marshall Plan was passed by Congress, on a Sunday evening, May 2, 1948, the Trenton Catholic German Club was having a musical evening to support the German War Relief. On the left hand side you will see "Geo Beichl's Zither Group" was playing. Admission was $1.20 (tax included).

THE TRENTON CATHOLIC GERMAN CLUB
PRESENTS A
GESELLSCHAFTSABEND
GERMAN MUSIC AND ENTERTAINMENT—CABARET STYLE

MASTER OF CEREMONIES
OTTO DOEDERLEIN

MAXWELL GIEDLIN'S
GERMAN-AMERICAN SPECIALTY BAND

G.T.V. "ALMRAUSCH"
TYROLIAN SOCIETY
IN TRADITIONAL DANCES

FAIRMOUNT LIEDERTAFEL'S
SCHARZEHAND QUARTET

GEO. BEICHL'S
ZITHER GROUP

DANCING

GIRLS OF ST. STEPHENS
IN
HUNGARIAN FOLK DANCES

H. VON THADEN
AND HIS
CONCERTINA
ENTERTAINER

ROSEMARIE KUNDEL
ARTISTE OF
THE ACCORDION

DANCING

G.T.V. "ALMRAUSCH"
OF PHILADELPHIA

Sunday Evening, May 2nd, 1948   **7:30 P.M.**

TRENTON CATHOLIC GYM 500 Chestnut Ave.   **ADMISSION $1.20** TAX INCLUDED

ALL PROCEEDS FOR GERMAN WAR RELIEF

TICKETS AVAILABLE AT TRENTON CATHOLIC or

Giving Back: Family, Prayer, Teaching, Repairing German American Relations

8. Starting a Family, Returning to Munich

MANY MEN, HAVING EXPERIENCED HARDSHIPS AND TRIALS IN LIFE, ARE often irrevocably hardened by them. They carry scars and may harbor ill will towards those who were disbelieving or cruel. The US Army put George in the Infantry and sent him to fight on foreign soil in spite of his advanced chemistry background and the need for chemists. They questioned his patriotism because of his membership in a German singing group. They informed his mother he was killed in action, and she put an obituary in the local newspaper. And from the enemy side, the German soldiers kept him captive, tried to get him to defect to their side, and they packed him into boxcars with fellow soldiers rather than release them when the war was surely close to an end.

George returned to his civilian status. And as he began the second half of his life, his loyalty to the US, his faith in the Lord, and his continued appreciation of his German heritage opened up his life's pathway, not only to marry, raise a family, and to teach, but also to repair broken relationships across the cultural divide.

Life moved on.

George met Isabella Lass after the war. She was born in Philadelphia to immigrant parents. They were married in 1951.

...there was a dance which enabled members of the audience to dance with the students. I recall dancing with one of the Austrian students who told me she was majoring in English and History. However, what struck me as strange when I asked her about Egon Friedell, the author of an interesting book, "The Cultural History of the Modern Age" she did not seem to be familiar with him or his book. Actually, he was Jewish and committed suicide when the Nazi troops occupied Vienna.

After the students left Philadelphia I had occasion to meet this "student" again.

Oddly enough, the Franklin Institute had scheduled a visit by a group of Swiss singers and musicians, which they had never done before.

I not only planned to attend the performance, but invited a cousin of my mother, Sepp Bernhart, to join me. He was a zither player who came to America and engaged himself as a boxer known as "Dutch Joe Bernhart, the Brooklyn Terror."

What was interesting was his arrival at the Franklin Institute that he brought along the young girl with whom I had danced at one of the concerts and who had not heard of Egon Friedell.

Puzzled I asked her why she had not gone back to Vienna when the students from Austria left. She confessed that she was not a student but went along with them whenever they performed at a German club.

This girl was Isabella Lass whom I dated from that time on and who I eventually married in 1951.

We had much in common. We spoke German dialects that were similar (Bavarian and Austrian) and were proud of our German-Austrian heritage.

Isabella was an accomplished musician, piano and keyboard, who knew many Viennese songs that she taught me.

We were married in St. Martin of Tours Church by Father Joseph Molloy, SJ, Chairman of the Chemistry Department at St. Joseph's College.

We had four children—Isabel, Karen, Christine, and Lisa. All of them learned to speak German, attending the language classes offered by the Danube Swabian Society.

At night she would say to me, "Angenehmes Flohbeissen" or "may you have a pleasant night of flea biting" which she must have learned from her Burgenland relatives. This is still our good night greeting.

—George Beichl

George enjoyed teaching in the lab at St. Joe's, and he also enjoyed his family life, as you can see him playing the zither, with his two older daughters, Isabel and Karen accompanying him on percussion and flute.

FROM A YELLOW PAD OF PAPER—In 1959 I received a National Science Fellowship (NSF) to the Inorganic Chemistry Institute of the University of Munich. Isabel, Karen and Christine joined us (Lisa was not born then). Isabel attended the Volkschule on Adalbertstrasse. Her teacher praised her "mastery" of German—she did not speak the dialect. Karen attended kindergarten.

Our parish was St. Ludwig's on the Leopoldstrasse, where the priest often gave the sermons. There were always some attendees who left Church after the sermon. They came just to listen to him.

Isabella, the children and I enjoyed the Munich celebration of Fasching (Mardi Gras). We attended several of the Faschingsparties in costume.

My mother's sister, Appolonia Gmas, lived in Munich and we often visited her, Tante Loni and her husband Onkel Pepe.

I learned much Inorganic Chemistry there that enabled me to prepare good courses in the subject when I returned to the US.

I also became good friends with Professor Ernst Otto Fischer who taught courses at the University and who was on the staff of the Technische Hochschule of Munich and went on to win the Nobel Prize in Chemistry (in 1973) for his experiments with sandwich compounds. I later invited him to give a talk at the Philadelphia American Chemistry Society section meeting.

When we returned to America, Isabella and I played music for sing-alongs at local retirement homes for the senior citizens, Isabella on the keyboard and I on the zither. We played songs that they all knew, e.g., "Let the rest of the world go by," and one they all recalled, "Yes we have no bananas."

I learned many Viennese songs from Isabella. This is a unique genre of German songs. Typical of these songs is:

> *Im Himmel spielt leise ein Schrammel Quartett*
> *Zwei Engerln aus Grinzing, dö singen Duett*
> *Dö singen von Liebe von Wien und vom Wein*
> *Der Petrus als Wirt schenkt den Heurigen ein.*

Dann spiel'n gar an Walzer von Lanner und Strauss
Es tanzt alles mit
Es hält kaner aus
Der Herrgott schaut zua und summt vor sich hin
Es gibt auch im Himmel ein Wien"

Which can be loosely rendered in English as "In heaven a Schrammel Quartet is playing softly. Two angels from Grinzing are singing duet. They sing about love, about Vienna, and wine. St. Peter as host is dispensing the new wine. Then they even play a waltz from Lanner and Strauss. Everyone joins in dancing since no one can resist. Our Lord looks on and hums to himself, 'There is a Vienna in heaven too.'"

Back in the US I developed a graduate course in Inorganic Chemistry at St. Joe's—Group Theory—as applied to the shapes of molecules, and gave lessons on the zither, and got the local zither players to give concerts.

—George Beichl

While they were in Germany, George was eager to see his former prison guard and lifelong friend, Karl Schäfer, again.

So he arranged a visit.

Though they remained in contact over the years through the packages George and his mother sent and through correspondence, the prisoner and guard had not seen each other since 1945. Mutual gratitude and friendship formed the foundation for a lifelong bond.

"I visited Karl Schäfer in Trier who tried to gain me access to the prison. However access was denied by the French military who used it as a military prison."

—George Beichl, 1984

Wittlich Prison was used to house French war criminals after the war, Nazi prisoners who were awaiting trials or serving their sentence.[109] The French held 19 war criminals in Wittlich Prison in 1955.[110]

Even the local newspaper appreciated the historical value of this friendship contrasted against a dark and horrifying war.

KRIEGSGEFANGENER UND WACHMANN TRAFEN SICH WIEDER

Amerikanischer Dozent von Philadelphia besuchte seinen Gefangenen-Posten von 1945

Bei der Ardennen-Offensive 1944 war der amerikanische Soldat Beichl aus Philadelphia gefangengenommen worden. Man brachte ihn in das Lager Wittlich. Geraume Zeit weilte er in einer Zelle des Gefängnisses. 1945 gab man Kriegsgefangene für den Außendienst in deutschen Betrieben frei.

Auf diese Weise kam Beichl als Weinbergsarbeiter aus "dem Bau" ins Freie.

Die Verpflegung war damals im Gefängnis schlecht. Durch die wankende Lage war schon damals im Grenzraum die Verpflegung der Zivilbevölkerung in Gefahr geraten. Als Beichl eines Tages wieder fuer ein Arbeitskommando abgeholt wurde, klagte er—da er perfekt deutsch sprach—über schlechtes Befinden. Der Wachmann nahm ihn nun mit nach Hause, wo seine Frau dem Amerikaner Tee bereitete und ihm zu essen gab. Mann und Frau nahmen sich des Kranken an und pflegten ihn. Schließlich nahte die Front—wenn man noch von einer solchen sprechen konnte—dem Raum Wittlich. Die Kriegsgefangenen wurden über den Rhein gebracht. Beichl kam nach Limburg, dann nach Gießen, wo er von seinen Landsleuten befreit wurde.

Die liebevolle Behandlung in Wittlich hat der ehemalige Kriegsgefangene nicht vergessen. Er schickte seinem Wachmann gleich nach dem Kriege, als in Deutschland praktisch Hungersnot herrschte, laufend Pakete. Und nun kam er selbst über den Atlantik. Der Prisoner von damals ist heute der Dozent Dr. Georg Beichl von der Universität Philadelphia. Er weilt mit einem Auftrag in Deutschland und studiert in München die deutsche Unterrichtsmethode an der Universität. Dr. Beichl ist Dozent für Chemie. Sein Wachmann von einst heißt Karl Schäfer und wohnt in Trier, Mustorstraße 3. Wachmann und Dozent sind heute per du und gute Freunde, eine Freundschaft die beide Familien umspannt. Denn Dr. Beichl brachte seine Familie mit "über den großen Teich." Gestern weilte er in Wittlich, um sich seine Haftanstalt von damals wieder anzusehen. Dabei wurde das Familienalbum von Philadelphia um einige Fotos reicher.

PRISONER OF WAR AND GUARD MEET AGAIN

American lecturer from Philadelphia visits 1945 prison post.

During the Ardennes Offensive in 1945 the American soldier, Beichl, from Philadelphia was taken prisoner. He was brought to Camp Wittlich, where he lived confined to a prison cell for some time. However, in 1945 some prisoners were allowed to participate in work duty outside the camp.

Thus, Beichl came to work in the vineyards outside the prison camp. The camp provisions were bad in those days. Because of the unstable situation, the food provisions of the civilian population in the border regions had become endangered. One day, when Beichl was again selected for work detail, he -who spoke perfect German-, mentioned that he did not feel well. The guard took him home where his wife prepared him tea and gave him some food. Husband and wife took care of the sick man and nursed him back to health. Finally the front—if one could still call it that—came closer to Wittlich. The prisoners of war were taken across the river, Rhine. Beichl was taken first to Limburg and then to Gießen, where he was freed by his countrymen.

The former prisoner of war did not forget the loving treatment he received in Wittlich. Soon after the war, because of the ongoing famine in Germany, he continuously sent his guard packages with food and essentials. And now he came himself over the Atlantic. The former prisoner is now the lecturer, Dr. George Beichl, at the University in Philadelphia. He was sent here to study the German methods of teaching at the University of Munich. Dr. Beichl lectures in Chemistry. His guard is Karl Schäfer and lives in Trier, Mustorstraße 3. Guard and lecturer are now good friends, a friendship that encompasses both families. Dr. Beichl brought his family with him "across the big pond." Yesterday, he was in Wittlich to see his former prison. Here, the family album from Philadelphia was enriched with some new photos.

Indeed it was.

9. Advancing German American relations, Prayer, Awards for teaching

THE INCONGRUENCE OF COMPASSIONATE GERMANS JUXTAPOSED AGAINST the horrors and atrocities committed during WWII created a complex country profile. George recognized the sensitivity of the German-Nazi lineage, and he believed that the Nazis were wrong on every level. He recognized that there were both hateful, prejudicial beliefs held by some Germans and open and loving philosophies held by other Germans. He also believed people could be redeemed and that hate in hearts could be displaced by love.

The work he completed to advance and improve the relations between Germany and America was significant. So much so that the German government awarded him two merits: das Verdienstkreuz and das Grosse Verdienstkreuz (Commander's Cross), the latter of which is said to be the highest honor that a non-German can be awarded. Past recipients include Norman Schwarzkopf.

FROM A YELLOW PAD OF PAPER—In 1983 we celebrated the 200th anniversary of the first German settlement in America, Germantown, by immigrants from Krefeld under the leadership of Daniel Pastorius. As President of the German Society of Pennsylvania, I presided at a formal banquet at which the President of Germany and Professor E. Otto Fischer (Nobel Prize winner in Chemistry in 1973, and someone he met during his sabbatical in Munich in 1959) attended. For the music the Munich Zither Trio came (Hannes and Robert Popp and Lothar Laegel).

—George Beichl

*

To give you an idea of his efforts, in 1983 he arranged for members of the Mummers South Philadelphia String Band to travel to Krefeld Germany to celebrate the 200-year anniversary of the first German families in Philadelphia (what is Germantown today). The Mummers are a unique Philadelphia tradition whose bands march up Broad Street on New Years' Day, playing banjos and saxophones and strutting with their ornately feathered costumes. Finding transportation not only for the Mummers but also for the voluminous costumes that can be up to 10 feet tall was complicated, but he was able to manage it.

He also wrote letters to the editor to present a different perspective. Here is one from Friday, April 26, 1985.

THE GERMAN SIDE SHOULD BE TOLD...

Friday, April 26,1985
By George J Beichl

Headlines emblazoned on the front of The Inquirer announced for several days the President's intention to visit a "Nazi" cemetery. Leaders of the Jewish community have besieged the White House asking him to desist from this visit. Columnist after columnist joins them in expressing their chagrin that a President would be so insensitive to the horrors of the Holocaust that he would lay a wreath to honor the Nazi dead, the perpetrators of the Holocaust. Yet not one word is printed that presents an opposing view, least of all from a member of the German American community, one of the largest, if not the largest, ethnic groups in our country.

To call the German military cemetery a "Nazi" cemetery is in keeping with media usage of equating Germans with Nazis that has been absorbed into the consciousness of many, if not most, Americans. I once overheard a high school student who had come upon a Mennonite family in Center

City, conversing in the Pennsylvania German dialect, tell her companion, "They're talking Nazi."

You knew that she meant "German" but you also knew how she and/ or her teachers felt about Germans just as you would know how people feel about Catholics if they were to label a Catholic cemetery, a "Papist" cemetery.

It is customary for visiting dignitaries to lay wreaths on the graves of fallen soldiers, even though those soldiers had fought against the country of the wreath-layer. It emphasizes not only a reconciliation—we are not enemies for all eternity—but also a recognition that those who died in combat were serving their country and were, for the most part draftees.

The modern state, even a democracy such as ours, could never survive if it could not depend on the blind loyalty of its citizens, even if they disagreed with the foreign policies of their country.

But, the rejoinder is made, the cemetery at Bitburg contains graves of the Waffen SS who were notorious for their ruthlessness. The SS, which started out as an elite group of volunteers, eventually had to have its ranks filled by draftees.

These were obtained from the air force and navy when these services were no longer operative. Even within the ranks of the regular SS were individuals, who, at great risk to themselves, tried to help the victims they were commanded to brutalize. At least one SS man is memorialized in the Yad Vashem, the institution in Israel dedicated to the Holocaust.

The President should visit the German cemetery at Bitburg. In doing this he would be giving public recognition to a government that from its inception in the ruins of World War II has seen to it that restitution for the crimes of the National Socialists was implemented.

How many Americans know that the German government has paid more than 50 billion marks to victims of the Nazi Holocaust in addition to more than three billion marks paid to Israel directly, in recognition of the fact that Israel had assumed a tremendous financial burden in accepting so many victims of Nazi oppression?

The President should visit the German cemetery at Bitburg. It would be a tribute to the many Germans who fought the Nazi regime and whose exploits are known to only a miniscule minority. How many know that the Lutheran theologian Dietrich Bonhoeffer, executed in 1945, could have saved his life by staying in the United States in the summer of 1939 but opted to return to Germany because he felt that he could not be in a position to participate in the reconstruction of Germany after the war if he did not share the hardship of this period with his people?

How many know that over 1,000 religious died or were executed at Dachau for resisting the regime? Among these was Father Bernhard Lichtenberg, provost of St. Hedwig's Cathedral in Berlin, whose treasonous act consisted in asking the congregation to pray for the Jews during a service in 1941. How many know that a German industrialist, Oskar Schindler, saved more than 1,000 Jews from Auschwitz in 1944 by moving his entire "labor camp" from Poland to Czechoslovakia, or that another German industrialist, Eduard Schulte, at the risk of death for himself and his family informed Jewish leaders in Switzerland in 1942 of the reality of the "final solution" imploring them to publicize this to Roosevelt and Churchill?

Why are the Germans judged guilty for failing to overthrow a dictatorship that brought death to so many millions when no one upbraids the Soviets for not overthrowing the Stalin dictatorship that killed more than 25 million? Where are the voices accusing the Poles, the Soviets, the Czechs, the Hungarians, the Iranians and many more of cowardice for not overthrowing the dictatorships imposed on them today?

America is strong because its diverse ethnic groups have been able to incorporate the positive aspects of their traditions into our own and to ignore the hatreds that prevailed among the groups in their homelands. If we allow this hatred of Germans to continue, we not only will weaken the bonds to our strongest ally in Europe but we will weaken the bonds between all Americans and sow the seeds of discord here in America which can only benefit one group of people—those who want to see America destroyed. *(George J Beichl is president of the German Society of Pennsylvania)*

RETURNING A FLAG

In 1986, a Philadelphia journalist, Tom Fox, approached George about a flag he saw in an antique shop in the 69th Street Terminal in Philadelphia. Tom was interested in the flag, and recognized it was German. He described it as "a magnificently embroidered 4 by 4 foot flag ... taken from a tavern wall in Herbrechtigen by an overzealous American GI." George had the German Society purchase the flag and then set out to find its rightful owner. The story was that "(t)he Americans liberated the village on April 26, 1945. They were put up in das Gasthaus zum Hirsch, the old Tavern to the deer." Then the story continues, "(t)hat's where the American GI found it and took it home to America as a war souvenir. A 90 year old woman, dead now, of course, saw him take it from the case and put it in his Army bag. But what could she do? It was wartime and we were so helpless." One of those there to greet the flag's return said, "I carried the flag when it was presented to the Liederkranz *(singing club)* in 1928," he said, fighting off tears. "I cannot believe that it has come back home to us. It is a modern fairy tale..." The story had a happy ending and the flag now sits back where it belongs, in Herbrechtigen near Stuttgart.[111]

REACHING OUT

There was a letter found in George's files from Franz Oppenheimer dated November 2, 1988. Mr. Oppenheimer was born to Jewish parents September 7, 1919, in Mainz, Germany and moved to the United States in the 1930s during the Nazi rise. He graduated from the University of Chicago in 1942 and from Yale Law School in 1945. He settled in Washington with his wife in 1947.[112]

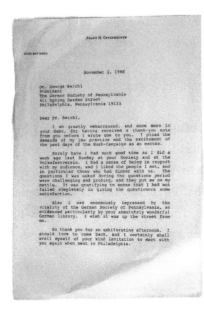
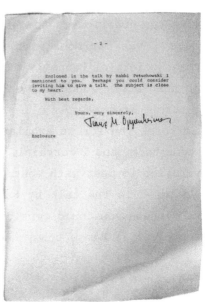

Franz M. Oppenheimer
November 2, 1988

Dear Dr. Beichl,

I am greatly embarrassed, and once more in your debt, for having received a thank-you note from you before I wrote one to you. I plead the demands of my law practice and the excitement of the past days of the Bush-Campaign as an excuse.

Rarely have I had such a good time as I did a week ago last Sunday at your Society and at the Volksfestverein. I had a sense of being in rapport with my audience, and I like the people I met, and in particular those who had dinner with us. The questions I was asked during the questions period were challenging and probing, and they put me on my mettle. It was gratifying to sense that I had not failed completely in giving the questioners some satisfaction.

Also I was enormously impressed by the vitality of the German Society of Pennsylvania, as evidenced particularly by your absolutely wonderful German library. I wish it was up the street from me.

So thank you for an exhilarating afternoon. I should love to come back, and I certainly shall avail myself of your kind invitation to meet with you again when next in Philadelphia.

Enclosed is the talk by Rabbi Petuchowski I mentioned to you. Perhaps you could consider inviting him to give a talk. The subject is close to my heart.

With best regards,
Yours, very sincerely, Franz M. Oppenheimer

Unfortunately, Rabbi Petuchowski's talk was not found with the letter. Jakob Josef Petuchowski passed away in 1991 at the early age of 66. He was a Reform Rabbi and a leader in Christian-Jewish dialogue who was the Sol and Arlene Bronstein professor of Judeo-Christian Studies at the Cincinnati campus of Hebrew Union College-Jewish Institute of Religion. He passed away due to pulmonary complications following bypass surgery.[113] He was born in Berlin, escaped Nazi Germany in 1939, and earned a bachelor's degree from the University of London. He was a prolific author of 36 books in Jewish theology and liturgy, including "Ever Since Sinai—a Modern View of Torah" (1961) and "The Lord's Prayer and Jewish Liturgy (1978)."

LIVING IN FAITH

An important thread in George's life was Catholicism. He went to Mass frequently, most often at Our Lady of Lourdes in Overbrook, and also at St. Peter the Apostle Church in the city. He treasured the chapel, particularly the shrine where St. John Neumann's body can still be seen. His daughter conveyed a story:

As my dad got older, when I was finally able to convince him to no longer drive, I would drive him to the chapel where there is a shrine to St. John Neumann. He liked to go to Confession there (when a person confesses sins and is then reconciled with the Church through penance of prayers) and then stay for Mass. I would usually walk in behind him, help him into the confessional and then stay for Mass with him.

On one of these trips, as I was driving him to the shrine he asked me if I would please go to Confession that day. I explained that I often talked and prayed to God and was ok not to go. A few minutes later, he asked again, saying he would consider it a favor. I replied the same answer as before. This went on during the entire car ride, so that by the time we arrived, I agreed.

After giving my confession to the priest, there was a pause. "Is that all?" the priest inquired. "Yes," I replied, "that's it." Another pause. "Is there anything you would like to talk about?" I said no, and then I realized, he was perhaps expecting a bigger bombshell than my sins of losing my patience with my elderly parents, or perhaps he was used to more of a conversation, I didn't know. So I explained that I had not intended to come to confession that day, "The truth is that my dad really wanted me to go to Confession, he's in the giant walker outside and is coming in right behind me. I don't have anything big to report, sorry to say." He laughed and gave me my penance (prayers to be said as an expression of repenting for something done wrong).

Prayer took many forms for George, including the Liturgy of the Hours, or Divine Office, or Breviary, which is the official set of prayers and readings that is obligatory for all Roman Catholic priests and deacons becoming priests to pray on a daily basis. There are four large volumes of prayers, readings, psalms, and together with the Mass, represent the official prayer life of the Church. There is a small pamphlet that comes out every year, letting individuals know which sets of prayers to say.

Recognizing the importance of prayer, George picked up a set of the prayer books at the St. Jude Shop in Havertown and began to say the prayers over the course of the day, every day. In spite of the huge size of these books, occasionally one would go missing. And over the years, the pages tore, so he ended up with about 3 incomplete sets at the end of his life.

But it wasn't just Mass and prayers to George; he lived his faith. For example, in the 1970s when Cesar Chavez was helping the farm workers unite, the family opened their home to Mexican farm-workers seeking improved workers rights. And if the family heard that an inner-city church had low attendance, they would participate in the Sunday Mass there. His daughter explained:

> I also remember as a young girl, my parents took us to different Catholic Churches in the city that had low attendance. One of my favorite Churches was Our Mother of Sorrows, whose pastor, Father Daly, was one of the kindest and gentlest men I have ever known.
>
> Our Mother of Sorrows was relatively close to our home, but the neighborhood was a little tough. The Mass was different from ours, and there were donuts afterwards, so you really couldn't lose.
>
> Father Daly did get into some trouble with the Church later in his life. As the only priest in the large rectory, he often let homeless sleep there. When the Church leadership found out about it, he was asked to stop. Which he did, and then he did it again. He lived his faith, too.

LEARNING AND TEACHING

George firmly believed in education, and he was always learning through reading and glad to teach anyone interested. From neighbors studying for a high school chemistry test to children interested in tutoring, the door was always open. In 1960, he received a letter from a very young chemist-to-be. It was addressed to Wanamaker's (a former department store) in downtown Philadelphia, where it appears George taught a Saturday morning chemistry course. This thoughtful letter describes how Michael and his friend Pat made some gunpowder that day and he was eager for George to send him a test to demonstrate his budding knowledge.

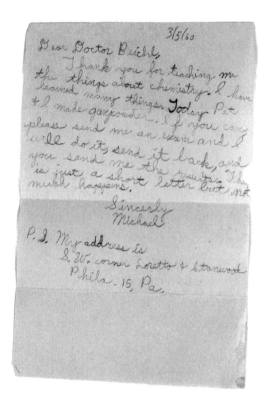

As a young girl, his daughter remembered George leaving before breakfast and when asked where he was going, her mother explained that he was tutoring some high school students in Chemistry. George also devoted his time to develop a summer lab program for inner-city youth to enable them to achieve college credits while in high school.

He was a demanding but fair teacher. As such, he was very engaged in the development of his students at St. Joe's. To this end, he donated more than 500 chemistry books to the library (and he still managed to have probably 1,000 left in his study on Drexel Road). He was given an honorary doctorate after the 1989 academic year, which was the last year that he taught. In 1990, he earned one of the University's top service-oriented accolades, the Rev. Joseph S. Hogan, S.J., Award. George taught thousands of students during his tenure, and the scope of his impact is immeasurable.

One of his former students in the 1960s, S. Robert Freedman, enrolled at St Joe's as a pre-med major and had George for inorganic chemistry. In testament to his impact, Dr. Freedman established the Herbert I and Shirley W Freedman Scholarship Fund to memorialize his parents and honor him. The fund will assist qualified St. Joseph's University chemistry students in perpetuity.[114] As his daughter explained:

My dad didn't say anything to anyone. In fact, I didn't know about the endowment until some phone calls started to come at home for him. After hearing the phone ring and ring, I asked my dad what it was about and he told me. Then I asked him how well he remembered Dr. Freedman and he responded to me, that Dr. Freedman was one of the smartest men he had ever met and that he didn't need a teacher at all, just someone to bounce ideas off of.

Of course, that's exactly what my dad would say, I need not have even asked.

10. Letters

"We are not human beings having a spiritual existence. We are spiritual beings having a human experience."

—Pierre Teilhard de Chardin

THE DETAILED DIARIES FROM 1939 AND FROM 1945 ALLOWED US TO SEE and experience Germany through George's eyes. He used his pen and pencil to process his experiences so that he could remember them, be reminded of that moment, and to reflect on the experience over time. Writing was an important medium, not only through his diaries, but also through his essays, and very much through letters.

He wrote letters generously.

He wrote them to friends, to family, to students, to neighbors, even to the newspaper delivery man. Through this medium, he let you know he was thinking of you, praying for you, appreciating you, asking you for help, thanking you, and so on.

Dr. Tim Cooke, son of Dr. Don Cooke (founding member of the Royal Knights of the Keg) studied Chemistry as an undergraduate at St. Joe's College and went on for his Ph.D. in Chemistry at Columbia. Here's a note that he wrote to Tim one summer:

July 12, 1979

Dear Tim, Thank you for your note indicating that you are enjoying a summer of research in Baker Lab high above Cayuga's waters. We will look forward to your description of this work via a seminar which we will start in the fall semester. Now there will be no excuse for conflicts on Thursday afternoons since the only labs scheduled will be General Chemistry.

By the way we have arranged for you to be a teaching assistant in the General Chem Lab. Tentatively they are scheduled for Tuesday and Friday afternoons. I assume you will also be available for the Motivation labs on Saturday morning. If not, let me know. Work hard in the labs but find time to relax afterward. Best regards to your mother and father and the girls and Buff and Pete.

Just received a call from North Jersey. Christine has another little girl.

Best regards, from your uncle, the department chairman

And here are some letters to his daughter Lisa when she was a student at Loyola College in Maryland.

1981

Dear Lisa,

Thank you for your wonderful letter in which you shared with us your feelings.

You pointed out the difficulty in growing up. This is a problem we all have to contend with. I think you are doing admirably. You have been exposed to many trying experiences. This is good for you because it makes you aware of the nature of the world you live in. Life consists of many problems. How you react to problems determines how you will enjoy life in the future. By recognizing a problem you make it easier when it comes again.

No one can respond to advice. We all have to learn by trial and error. Once you have suffered from an incident it leaves a deep impression on your psyche. I am impressed and grateful for the ways in which you have met the problems that beset you.

I often think of the quotation from St. John's Gospel, "You have not chosen me. I have chosen you. Go and bear fruit that will last" and I wonder where is the permanent fruit that will last from our marriage. When I see how you are developing I know that you will be the "permanent fruit" that will carry love into your environment.

You can't do it alone. You need to feel the presence of our Lord in your life and you need to associate with people who are filled with the Lord.

Don't worry about your exams. You have worked hard and that is all that is asked of you. Love, Dad

10/17/82

Dear Lisa,

Both of us are now starting the second quarter. I must admit it is easier for me than for you. When you are a student you have to stay up late studying for exams, and writing papers. As a result you start the next quarter exhausted.

It would be a good idea if you could catch up with your

sleep and get your exercise back on schedule as soon as possible so that you can benefit from the 2nd quarter.

I have no particular purpose in writing other than to say "Hello." It so happens that I got up early today, 4:30 am, and this is the best time to write.

My papers are marked and my grades are in. Unfortunately I have some low grades, about 5 or 6 F's. Most of these low grades arise because of poor arithmetic ability. Students don't know whether to divide or multiply. This is one of the sad products of introducing so-called "Modern Math" into grammar schools. Some years ago the top mathematicians in the country drew up a formal protest that urged that the "Modern Math" program be scrapped. Hopefully this been done and eventually a new generation will come on to campus that has mastered arithmetic.

As you start the new quarter, start reading the books assigned to you so that you can complete the reports on them early. This will allow you more time to study for your semester exams.

Are you in any extracurricular activities outside of the magazine? Do they have a Glee Club? This is always a good activity especially if the club visits other schools to give concerts.

By the way I came across an interesting quotation that I recommend. It was quoted by Dr. Satillaro, who wrote a book "Recalled by Life" in which he describes the healing of a bone cancer that he experienced. He is head of Methodist Hospital in South Philly. The quote is, "Let us keep this truth before us. You say you have no faith? Love—and faith will come. You say you are sad? Love—and joy will come. You say you are alone? Love—and you will break out of your solitude. You say you are in hell? Love—and you will find yourself in heaven. Heaven is love. "

Write when you get a chance. Love, Dad

1983

Dear Lisa,

I rarely have a chance to talk to you outside of the
fleeting moments that we talk on the telephone.

I know that course work is hard. However that is the way
you learn. Unless you are forced to study, you do not do
it. Thus, if you want to learn a language, you have to take
a course or go to the country where the language is spoken.

Just keep up the steady application. At the end of the
semester you will note that you have learned much. Eventually

you will learn to teach yourself, which is, or should be, the goal of all education.

But education is more than learning course material. You also have to learn how to judge people and how to treat different kinds of people. Don't be intimidated by those who flaunt their knowledge. They have an inferiority complex and need to show some superiority.

Find people who can love, both men and women. Don't confuse love with self-love. Many people seem to be affectionate but they want self-gratification. A person who loves will make sacrifices so that the person he loves can be happy.

Naturally that means that you must be loving. Help people, especially those who can't help you. This will enable you to find a husband to whom you can commit yourself for life. You may just find someone who is also helping others. Love, Dad

His letters continued over the years.

February 1, 2005

Dear Lisa,

I have been meaning to write for some time. I want you to know that you are in my prayers daily. What I want you to know is that you too, must put yourself in the Lord's hands and be alert to what opportunities he gives you.

We often refer to serendipitous events in our lives. The word, serendipity, is derived from the ancient name of Ceylon— Serendip. There is a tale that refers to three princes of

Serendip who came upon treasures that they were not looking for.

Christians have the added advantage that they can pray to the Lord to put things and people in their path that will enable them to accomplish the objectives that they seek.

Then at the end… You will be surprised by what you will encounter serendipitously. We will be in touch with you regularly. Love, Dad

Towards the end of his life, he continued to write letters; these were more of thanks. Here's one he wrote when he was 93 years old:

January 1, 2011

Dear Lisa,

I wanted to write you this letter before Christmas but never did until now.

I want you to know that I appreciate all that you have done for mother and for me.

Among your other talents, you are an excellent cook. I am grateful not only for the holiday dinners, but all of your meals, spaghetti and meatballs, omelets…

In addition, you see to it that I have clean, dry clothes despite my incontinence. I appreciate your folding my undershirts which I have tried and found hard to do. In addition your shopping has been a boon to us. You have gone out of your way to take me to Sears for my Hearing Aids. You even learned to repair them and did so on several occasions.

You took me to the Ear Nose and Throat Doctor and then

bought the humidifiers and saw to it that they functioned properly. You took me to see Dr. Turchi at Fitz.

In addition you found a solution to my VA eligibility and drove to Port Richmond to visit Representative Brady's assistant. This, despite your work in preparing a new course for your trip to the Republic of Georgia and working on the development of a tool that would provide you with a permanent income. You have gotten workers to repair problem areas in our home, e.g., the downspouts on the roof.

You have sacrificed your time to get your mother and me to a variety of places including Church, the German Society, and mother's hairdresser.

In addition you have persevered in learning to play the bagpipe.

The Lord knows all that you have done for us and will bless your work with success.

I want you to know that I am grateful for what you have done and pray for you daily. You are a great woman. Sincerely, Dad

11. The Veterans Administration, medals, and more letters

"Never in the field of human conflict was so much owed by so many to so few."—Winston Churchill

When George was accepted into in-home hospice care, he became friends with the Director of the Veterans Advisory Commission, Scott Brown.

It was serendipitous.

Upon learning the details of his war experience, Scott was surprised that George had not received any medals for his service and so he set about the difficult task of procuring them. As a result of his efforts, in May 2014, at City Hall in Philadelphia, George was awarded the Combat Infantryman's Badge, the Bronze Star, the Purple Heart, the Prisoner of War Medal, the WWII Victory medal, the European-African-Middle Eastern Campaign Medal, the Good Conduct Medal, and the WWII American Campaign Medal.

He received letters that he responded to:

Draft letter from June 23, 2014 from a yellow pad of paper
Dear Treau,

Many thanks for your kind letter congratulating me for my military service. Actually the only student I have had with the name Treau is Treau Kobelak and I never forgot her.

Actually my mother, a widow, received a telegram from the War Department announcing that I had been killed in action. I had been captured by the Germans and my mother was informed that I was a POW. I was later released and this status was made known to my family.

You were fortunate in having had Dr. Alan MacDiarmid as your professor of Inorganic Chemistry at the University of Pennsylvania. The FDA was fortunate to have had you on their staff of problem solvers.

May you continue to thrive as a problem solver in the chemistry profession.

Sincerely,

And then St. Joseph's University put an article in the Alumni Magazine about George's Wartime experience.[115] He received a number of letters in response. Here are a few:

October 10, 2014

Dear Dr. Beichl,

I recently read the article about you in the Fall issue of SJU Magazine and thought I would like to send you a long overdue thank you for your excellent advice, guidance, and classroom teaching. You will not remember me as I was not outstanding in any particular way, but you were my academic advisor and organic chemistry professor as well as my laboratory teacher during my time at St. Joe's graduate evening school until my graduation in 1979.

I learned more from you than from all my other classes combined. You were patient, easy to talk to, and eminently knowledgeable about all aspects of chemistry. I know I was extremely fortunate to have had you contribute to my education.

Thank you so much for everything!

God Bless!

Sincerely, David Pliner

October 10, 2014

Dear Dr. Beichl,

I have just received the Fall 2014 SJU Magazine and saw the article on the recent and not so recent events in your life. I felt I had to write to congratulate you.

I'm sure you don't remember me, but I certainly remember you and the impact you had on my career. We first met in 1962 (the class of 1966). I was a Chemistry major along with other students from my High School (Bishop Neumann), Frank Caputo and Sal Pizzo. We were typical students at the College at the time, first generation college students from blue-collar backgrounds. In addition to the course work and the formal education, I needed advice and mentoring and you supplied it whether you realized it or not. I wasn't a particularly good student because I worked an outside job every opportunity I could, but the education I received was second to none. Your advice was simple and direct, work hard and maintain a positive attitude. You helped me plan my graduate career and that advice helped me to go on to graduate school.

I eventually went to graduate school at Virginia Tech, then called VPI. I received an Atomic Energy Commission Traineeship and worked at Brookhaven National Lab on Long Island. My research areas were Hot Atom Chemistry and use of positron annihilation to study electron density in chemical reactions. I finished my research in 1971 and received my PhD in Chemistry in 1972. The next 18 years I spent as head of the Police Criminalistics Lab for the City of Philadelphia. I left there and worked at the Smithsonian Institution for another 16 years working on some of the most interesting questions a chemist could hope for. I retired from the Smithsonian in 2006 and after a brief period started working at the University of Baltimore and at present I am Head of the Forensic Studies Program at the University. I hope I help my students as much as you helped yours.

You were responsible for my first job after graduation from St. Joe's. It was an error however. An acquaintance of yours told you to tell Charlie to apply at Allied Chemical for a job and he would vouch for him. You told me and I went and got the job except that the Charlie he referred to was Charlie Bracken and not me! Charlie actually wound up working for the Drug Analysis section in the Police Lab, but unfortunately passed away from MS some years ago.

I remember your General Chemistry course vividly and even the first year glassblowing course with a lot of burnt fingers. Drs. Koob and Di Carlo also rounded out my memories of hard but interesting courses.

As an aside, your insistence on German as a necessity for chemists led me to do some translating of 19th century German chemistry articles for my colleagues at the Smithsonian.

I hope this brings back fond memories of long-ago students and lets you know that with all your well-deserved public honors, there are students who honor you in their thoughts.

With warm regards, Charlie S. Tumosa

January 29, 2015

Sirs: I commend the edition of SJU Mag (Fall 2014) and Kristen A. Graham for the delightful tribute to Prof. George Beichl, PhD

As a student in 1948 Dr. B taught me, the pre-meds, and science people, basic inorganic chemistry. His course was structured, well organized, and presented with clarity and authority.

Many of his students are indebted to him for opening the door toward advanced organic and biochemistries.

His presence at the "College" for decades was a gift to many hundreds of students who subsequently achieved in their chosen destinies.

Many thanks for your time, effort, and expertise.

Gratefully, Louis Welsh MD, SJC '52

12. Saying Goodbye

"The most satisfying thing in life is to have been able to give a large part of one's self to others."—Pierre Teilhard de Chardin

George eventually found himself in a comfortable bed by a window at the Community Living Center in the Philadelphia VA. The small number of rooms in the Inpatient Hospice ensured genuine care and appropriate clinical attention. He had many visitors, including a long-distance musical guest and close family friend, Hannes Popp, an accomplished Bavarian zither player from Switzerland. Hannes held a zither concert at the German Society of Pennsylvania on Spring Garden Street in Philadelphia for George. And Scott organized a Veteran's Warrior Motorcycle escort. There Hannes played zither favorites, including the "Theme from the Third Man" by Anton Karas, "Der Weg zum Herzen" by Georg Freundorfer, and other beloved compositions.

The last few months of George's life were peaceful. His wife, four daughters and Scott (aka George Jr.) visited him regularly. They enjoyed their time with him through music, reading, talking, or just holding his hand. Friends from the German Society, including Kurt Maute, who George loved like a son, were often present.

Thanks to a recommendation from Bill McGarvey and Patty McGarvey Knebels, St. Joseph's Prep honored him with the "Alumnus of the Year" (2015) award for embodying the spirit of Jesuit tradition, including service to others, which he understood and was grateful and appreciative. They were aware of his beer enterprise in 1934 at the Prep, and gave him the award anyway.

Though George's strength was declining, he continued to smile and sing, even if "singing" meant just mouthing the words. And so he "sang" with the compassionate nurses from the VA Hospice unit who went out of their way to bring in German song sheets with words to great tunes, including Stille Nacht (Silent Night) and the Rogers and Hammerstein hit "Edelweiss."

His daughter recalled:

He left us early Friday morning, February 6, 2015. I received a call at 3:30 am and they let me know he had died.

When I arrived at the VA Hospice, his body was warm. I could still hold his hand, but for the first time in my life, he didn't hold it back.

While the family hoped to have his service at the Chapel at St. Joseph's University, it was not to be. Instead, the funeral was held on February 12, 2015 at Old St. Joseph's Church on Willings Alley. Old St. Joe's was the original home of St. Joe's College (now University). The homily was given by Rev. William J. Byron, S.J. and here are some of his words:

I first met George Beichl in a chemistry classroom at St. Joseph's College after the war. I was there on the G.I. Bill of Rights. I was trying to figure out what I wanted to do and soon found that science was not my strong suit, so I transferred to a pre-law program. I had no idea that he was a war hero and had been held by the Germans as a prisoner of war. Many of us in the student body at the College in those days—probably half—were veterans; they were great years of growth and discovery. The future was all out there in front of us. I joined the Jesuits in 1950. George stayed on at St. Joe's helping the college achieve university status and guiding the professional development of generations of future scientists and physicians. He was an outstanding teacher and dedicated mentor.

One of my Jesuit friends, Father Jim Salmon, a Navy veteran, came to Penn to study for a doctorate in chemistry while he was still a Jesuit scholastic, not yet ordained to the priesthood. I spoke to Jim the other day and he couldn't say enough by way of gratitude to George for helping him adjust to and succeed in graduate studies at Penn where George had done so well a decade or so earlier.

Toward the end, we know that George grew weary and found life burdensome, but as he knew so well from pondering the words of Jesus that all of us just heard again from Matthew's gospel, "(L) earn from me; for I am gentle and humble of heart. Your souls will find rest, for my yoke is easy and my burden light" (Mt.11:30). His soul has found rest but what does that mean?

A hymn that is part of a Night Prayer in the Liturgy of the Hours (the Divine Office of "Breviary," as it is sometimes called) says it nicely, "We praise you, Father, for your gifts/ Of dusk and nightfall over earth/ Foreshadowing the mystery/ of death that leads to <u>endless day</u>."

Endless day. That is George Beichl's experience now. He is now eternally awake and eternally aware. The English word "enthusiasm" comes from two Greek words "<u>en theos</u>" meaning "in God." And that is what George is experiencing now. We can only speculate on what eternal enthusiasm is like for him.

Endless day. Endless awareness, endless enthusiasm—<u>en theos</u>— in God. The George we knew as husband, father, Pop-Pop, friend, professor, mentor; the man of faith whose exemplary life inspired us all, was always alert and aware. It is comforting for us now to think of him as eternally alert and eternally aware, caught up to his eternal delight in the love of God. We pray to and for him now. We give thanks to God for the great gift he was to each of us."

Scott Brown from the VA provided a moving eulogy:

Doctor and I met by accident (or now as I have come to believe it was divine intervention). I had just started as Director, had come back from a meeting and had just sat down at my desk when the phone rang; answering the phone I was informed that this great

REPORTED KILLED IN ACTION

Veteran needed some help. The story floored me. Stopped me right in my tracks. I won't tell you word for word of our conversation but, that night I had to meet the Doctor and I did.

His life story teaches us to be humble; his life teaches us to suffer with dignity. He always believed in forgiving your persecutors. George lived Matthew, Chapter 5 V 10-12 "Blessed are those who have been persecuted for the sake of righteousness, for theirs is the kingdom of Heaven. Blessed are you when people insult and persecute you and falsely say all kinds of evil against you because of me. Rejoice and be glad for your reward in Heaven is great; for in the same way they persecuted the prophets who were before you."

When I asked George, "What I should say at your funeral", he looked up at me, smiled and said, "Well, Scott, tell the few people there to pray fervently and believe and to never judge people, just love them." Mother Teresa of Calcutta once said, "If you judge people, you have no time to love them."

In closing I will say this… George was a saint among us. We were lucky to have lived, worked, studied, and to have been a friend to such a man, such an American hero, such a holy human.

What a moment it must have been when God reached out his hand and grabbed George's. Job well done servant, come home.

There was a luncheon after the burial at the German Society. The sauerbraten was exceptional and Willi Aust played the accordion, including George's favorite song, "So Ein Tag":

So ein Tag, so wunderschön wie Heute,
So ein Tag, der dürfte nie vergehn.
So ein Tag, auf den man sich so freute,
Und wer weiss, wann wir uns wiedersehn.

Such a day as beautiful as today,
Such a day should never end.

Such a day to which we so look forward,
And who knows when we will meet again.

Many friends memorialized George, including Christel Tillmann, President of the Women's Auxiliary of the German Society of Pennsylvania:

I am here today to honor a truly great man and express my personal and the women's heartfelt sympathy to his family and friends.

An exceptional man has left us. Born 96 years ago here in Philadelphia to German immigrant parents, he was a true American proud of his German heritage, always pointing out how prominently and tightly the German element was interwoven into the colorful American fabric.

The women of the Auxiliary were one of his biggest fan clubs, and for good reason. He always pointed out how much the women contributed to the Society. I do not remember a single Auxiliary event when I did not receive a handwritten note afterwards, praising our accomplishments. He noticed the smallest details. For example, a few years ago, when we first started wearing name tags at the *Christkindlmarkt,* he noticed and thought it to be wonderful that now he could address even the newcomers by name.

Today, I would like to share my first encounter with Dr. Beichl.

45 years ago, when I came to America, I often had to defend my homeland in this country. Vividly, I remember one heated conversation about the Marshall plan and the accusation that none of the countries ever paid back their loans. I knew that Germany was making payments but did not know if they ever had paid the loan in its entirety. I asked Dr. Beichl and he promised he would look into it. Months later, I had long forgotten my request; I received a hand written note accompanied by the official documentation that the Germans had paid their loan back in full. This made a deep impression on me that a man of his stature would find the time to do the research for somebody he did not even know at that time.

When I thanked him I asked if there was anything I could do for him. He answered yes; you could become a member of the German Society. I am a Capricorn and you might know that people born under this sign do not make decisions on the spur of the moment. It took me a while to make up my mind, but a year or two later I signed up for membership.

Let me assure you, Dr. Beichl will not be forgotten as long as the German Society exists, and I hope this will be for another 250 years. He will greet all of us on the fourth floor on our way to the library.

In fact, the "Beichl Tower" (housing the elevator) was formally opened in 2010, and at that time, Christel and Ron Tillmann donated the portrait of him that now sits on the wall outside the Horner Library (the German Society of Pennsylvania's extensive library). Here is a speech that Christel gave at that time:

Today we are all here at the German Society to honor Dr. George Beichl, a man of substance, with the unveiling of his portrait. This will be prominently displayed on the wall across the elevator exit, here on the fourth floor, close to Dr. Beichl's favorite spot in the building, the Horner Memorial Library.

As long as I have been a member of the Society - and that's over 35 years - there has been talk of the need for an elevator, but funds for such a large undertaking always seemed to be needed more urgently for other purposes.

Finally, in 2006, two of Dr. Beichl's long-time friends, Hans Trustorff and Ulrich Both, stepped forward and offered the seed money for such a project. Ulrich is with us today. Unfortunately, Hans passed on before the project was completed, but I would like to welcome his widow, Liesl, and her family.

In June 2008, at the groundbreaking for the tower, I asked Hans what prompted him to make this generous pledge. Let me share with you now the answer he gave me: Some time ago, Hans said, Dr. Beichl had told him that, because of the many steps, he was no longer able to visit the library as often as he desired. Hans Trustoff saw an opportunity to repay an overdue debt. He said he never forgot that 40 years ago, when he started his company with Ulrich Both and they still had problems with the English language, it was George who helped them with their official correspondence, always willing, never asking for anything in return.

This action exactly portrays Dr. Beichl as <u>we</u> all know him and as he is known in the German-American community at large: Always willing to listen, always willing to offer his help, always ready to share his vast knowledge and, when not knowing something off-hand, researching the matter and then getting back with an answer.

After receiving his Bachelor of Science degree from St. Joseph's University in 1939, he and his mother decided to visit relatives in Germany and barely made it back to the United States due to the outbreak of the Second World War.

He started his 50-year teaching career at St Joseph's University in 1940 and received his Master of Science degree in 1942 followed by his Ph.D. in 1953, both from the University of Pennsylvania.

He was drafted into the US Army and was captured during the Battle of the Bulge and sent to a prison camp in Germany. His mother received notice that he was "killed in action" in Germany, which fortunately was not true. Upon his return to the US, he worked under Robert Oppenheimer with top scientists and researchers from various universities across the country on the Manhattan Project in Los Alamos, New Mexico.

When he received the National Science Foundation Faculty Fellowship Award at the University of Munich in 1958, he and his family decided to stay in Germany for 12 months.

In 1963, Dr. Beichl received the Lindback Award for Distinguished Teaching at St. Joseph's followed in 1979 by the

German Academic Exchange Service Award at the University of Munich.

In the German American community, Dr. Beichl is best known as President of our beloved German Society of Pennsylvania, the oldest German Society in America, where he served as President for 19 years.

During this time, he established and entertained excellent relationships with all German organizations, and he is widely respected for his contributions.

In 1977, Dr. Beichl joined with other leaders of the German American community in establishing the United German American Committee of the US, which is now the German American Heritage Foundation in Washington, D.C.[116]

He still serves on the Boards of both organizations as President Emeritus and Honorary Director, respectively.

In 1983, he was instrumental in organizing the Tricentennial Celebration of the arrival of the first German settlers here in Philadelphia, which was attended by then President Carstens of the Federal Republic of Germany and then Vice President Bush, Sr. of the United States.

The Federal Republic of Germany awarded Dr. Beichl with the Officers Cross of the Order of Merit (Bundesverdienstkreuz) in 1977, and he received the Commanders Cross (Grosses Verdienstkreuz) in 1983. In the same year, he was awarded the Founders Medal of The German Society of Pennsylvania.

Dr. George Beichl is a true American but proud of his German heritage, who never fails to point to the German element interwoven into the colorful American fabric. He lives by Goethe's adage "Was du ererbt von deinen Vätern hast, erwirb es, um es zu besitzen" which translates to "What you inherited from your fathers, you must earn in order to possess."

Thank you, Dr. Beichl, for the exemplary life of an American who honors his German ancestry.

Christel & Ron Tillmann
August 2010

After his death, the City Council of Philadelphia recognized and honored his legacy through legislation and expressed condolences.

Friends wrote sympathy letters that were deeply appreciated. This one from Doris Simon (a member of the German Society and of the Women's Auxiliary of the German Society, and the one person he could count on to bring him Springerle—a traditional German anise cookie—during the Christmas season) included a letter George wrote to her in 1990 regarding the loss of her mother.

Dear Lisa, I am enclosing a scanned copy of the letter I received from your dad a week after my mom died twenty-five years ago. Your dad's words in the first three paragraphs were so comforting to me that I wanted to share them with you in the hope that they bring comfort to you as well.

January 28, 1990
Dear Doris,

Words cannot resolve the grief that you feel. But they can let you know that your many friends realize the pain of loss that you are experiencing.

When our loved ones leave us, even though we know that they are going to a better life, we miss their presence. This is especially true of our mothers, who nurtured us from our birth, who shared our heartaches, who enjoyed with us those times when we had cause to be filled with joy. They supported us, too, when most people misunderstood us.

But their absence is but temporary. We will meet them again when they and we will no longer be threatened with sickness and death....

Cleaning out the house, more letters emerged. This last one to his daughter Lisa was still attached to the yellow pad of paper upon which it was written and a good way to end this story. Even at the end of his life, he continued to appreciate others.

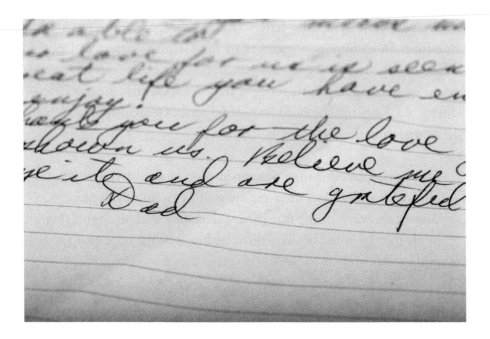

There is no gift that mother and I could give you that would correspond to the careful attention you have given mother and me that have made our final days on earth so wonderful, despite the time and attention you must pay to the professional demands of your job.

The Lord will bless you and compensate you more than we are able to.

Your love for us is seen in the great life you have enabled us to enjoy.

Thank you for the love you have shown us. Believe me, we recognize it and are grateful.

Dad

Always grateful, George lived his life in thanks, in confidence and in the present. Even when stranded in Munich in 1939, without funds to return home when WWII broke out, even as an educated scientist sent into the Infantry, and when captured in 1945 during WWII and taken as a prisoner in Germany, instead of bemoaning his fate, cursing the world, or feeling the level of frustration many of us would, he remained present, he looked for solutions, and he stayed true to his faith.

From a contemporary perspective, the diaries warn us never to underestimate the power of a dictatorship. If one is ever afraid to speak out about an accepted opinion, warning bells should signal high alert. We are wise to be wary of generalizations and careful not to judge those who closely associate with their culture. And if contentment is the goal, accepting life's circumstances while seeking solutions and experiencing the moment are probably the best routes to take.

While he was American to the core, George effectively and proudly wove the positive attributes of his German culture into the fabric of his life at a time when many struggled with the after effects of WWII, so much so that it was hard to see where one culture ended and the other began.

His character is seen through his behavior. He approached his education seriously. In fact, even though the trip to Munich in 1939 was intended to be a vacation, he preferred signing up for courses at the University. His diary documented voices in support of and opposition to National Socialism. He was interested in different viewpoints—from the Dane he met on a German train in 1939 who expressed concern regarding Germany's expansion in the north, to a Slovakian woman he met at a dance in Munich who believed Hitler was on the right track. He appreciated the generous friendship from his early prison guard and friend, Karl Schäfer, who risked his life to help him survive his early days as a POW. He treated all people with respect, even saluting the German Colonel after his final interrogation in the castle at Diez. After the boxcar bombings during the escape from Stalag XIIA, rather than leaving with the core group to find safety, he stayed behind with the wounded. Once they located a German doctor in a village, he performed simultaneous translations between the wounded GI's and the doctor. The translations included communicating current medical history, symptoms, and any clarifications the doctor required to correctly diagnose and treat. This decision led him to witness an unexpected confrontation between an angry SS officer and the compassionate German doctor. And in a surprising twist, rather than shooting the enemy soldiers on the spot, the SS officer led the German doctor away. As the war continued to rage on, he settled in to life as a chemist on the Manhattan Project. His confidence and optimism never wavered, so much so that even when socializing with fellow scientists on the weekends in Los Alamos, he had no compunction in leading the singing of German songs.

Perhaps most revealing of all, we would never have learned many of the rich, personal and historic details from either diary had the Philadelphia VA not mysteriously lost George's POW status in December 2010. Never boastful, the stories, experiences, names, places and details of the changing world would have remained safely tucked in George's memory; and the astonishing twists and turns of life that filled the pages of the unsuspecting diaries would have been relegated to a pile of books and letters collecting dust. After all, his personal diaries were never intended to be shared with anyone else.

His advice to his children was simple. Honor the Lord and lead a fulfilled life. Looking back, George honored the Lord in his loving, trusting, helping, learning, forgiving, defending and appreciating others. And these experiences brought him peace, joy, and fulfillment.

He often remarked, "I had a great life!" Even as his days on earth were slowly coming to an end, lying in the hospice bed by the window, his clear blue eyes smiled deeply as he gently squeezed his daughter's hand and whispered with genuine and heartfelt intent, "I *really* had a great life."

Indeed he did; though it might be more accurate to call it … *remarkable*.

Notes

1. The Commander's Cross is said to be the highest honor that the Federal Government of Germany can bestow upon a non-German.
2. The U.S. National Archives and Records Administration. "The 1973 Fire, National Personnel Records Center: The National Personnel Records Center (NPRC) Fire: A Study in Disaster," http://www.archives.gov/st-louis/military-personnel/fire-1973.html, (2015)
3. Winifried Nerdinger. Ed. *Munich and National Socialism – Catalogue of the Munich Documentation Centre for the History of National Socialism* (bookstore edition) (Munich: Verlag C.H. Beck oHG, 2015)
4. Traditional Islamic veil that women wear that covers the head and chest area.
5. "World War II," http://www.history.com/topics/world-war-ii, (2015)
6. "Battle of the Bulge December 1944," U.S. Army, http://www.army.mil/botb/, (2015)
7. Jenye Donaldson, "22nd Infantry National Memorial unveiled at Fort Benning," *Morning Reporter*, (June 23, 2015) http://raycomgroup.worldnow.com/story/29388793/22nd-infantry-national-memorial-unveiled-at-fort-benning
8. Girard College in Philadelphia was formed through the philanthropy of Stephen Girard (1750-1831) a French immigrant. The focus of Girard College was to educate poor, orphaned, or fatherless boys who would then live at the College and be educated, thereby providing a better chance of success in life.
9. The priest at St. Ludwig's offered that the nuns would help George's mother with childcare, and they did. And his mother would also send George down to the convent to help as well.
10. The zither is a traditional Bavarian stringed instrument (typically found in southern Germany and Alpine Europe), most commonly known through the movie *The Third Man*

11. "A German-American Chronology," http://maxkade.iupui.edu/adams/chrono. html (2015)

12. Department of Justice, Federal Bureau of Investigation, *Freedom of Information/ Privacy Acts Release. Subject: German American Bund,* https://vault.fbi.gov/ german-american-bund/german-american-federation-bund-part-11-of-10, (2015)

13. Willi Aust is a retired German teacher and a talented musician in the Philadelphia area. He plays the accordion for many German events, which included George's 90th birthday party and George's funeral lunch held at the German Society of Pennsylvania, 611 Spring Garden Street in Philadelphia.

14. *The New Yorker Staatszeitung* was founded in 1834. It's a weekly newspaper still in publication owned by Jes Rau.

15. The Women's Auxiliary of the German Society of Pennsylvania (WAUX) is still very active. The group supports charity and education as well as artistic and cultural events.

16. Department of Justice, Federal Bureau of Investigation, *Freedom of Information/ Privacy Acts Release. Subject: German American Bund,* https://vault.fbi.gov/ german-american-bund/german-american-federation-bund-part-11-of-10, (2015)

17. Ibid

18. Central Intelligence Agency (CIA), "A Look Back ... Marlene Dietrich: Singing for a Cause," https://www.cia.gov/news-information/featured-story-archive/2008-featured-story-archive/marlene-dietrich.html, (2015)

19. Ibid

20. Reichsmarks were the currency in use in 1939 Germany

21. Though he wrote 24 slain Nazis, this refers to the failed Beer Hall Putsch by Hitler to overthrow the government. Deaths were reported at 16 and those slain were considered martyrs by the Nazi Party.

22. Mark Weber, "How Hitler Tackled Unemployment and Revived Germany's Economy," *Institute for Historical Review,* http://www.ihr.org/other/ economyhitler2011.html (2015)

23. The "Munich Child" is the name of the city symbol on its coat of arms. "Drauf" refers to 'on it.'

24. Typical Bavarian dresses with colorful flowers or polka dots, worn with an apron.

25. American Museum of Natural History, "The Manhattan Project," http://www.amnh.org/exhibitions/past-exhibitions/einstein/peace-and-war/the-manhattan-project (2015)

26. International Herald Tribune, New York Herald Tribune, "1939: Reporter Doesn't Expect War," July 1, 1939 http://iht-retrospective.blogs.nytimes.com/2014/06/30/1939-reporter-doesnt-expect-war/?_r=0 (2015)

27. US Department of State – Office of the Historian, Milestones: 1914-1920 "The Paris Peace Conference and the Treaty of Versailles," https://history.state.gov/milestones/1914-1920/paris-peace (2015)

28. German History in Documents and Images (GHDI), "Documents – Beginnings: War and Revolution," http://germanhistorydocs.ghi-dc.org/sub_document.cfm?document_id=3829, (2015)

29. Martin Kitchen, BBC, "The Ending of World War One, and the Legacy of Peace," http://www.bbc.co.uk/history/worldwars/wwone/war_end_01.shtml (2015)

30. Kircher was a 17th century German Jesuit scholar.

31. This movie, starring Brigitte Horney, Willy Bergel, and Hannelore Schroth tells the story about a beautiful woman, Maria, whose life changes after a ball where she becomes acquainted with a senior officer (The Gouveneur) whom she marries.

32. Reinhard Siegmund-Schultze, "Mathematicians Fleeing from Nazi Germany: Individual Fates and Global Impact," (New Jersey: Princeton University Press 2009), p 53.

33. The Editors of Encyclopaedia Britannica, Encyclopaedia Britannica, "Salomon Bochner American Mathematician," http://www.britannica.com/biography/Salomon-Bochner (2015)

34. Christopher Hutton, *Linguistics and the Third Reich: Mother-tongue Fascism, Race and the Science of Language,* (London: Routledge, October 12, 2012)

35. Winifried Nerdinger. Ed. *Munich and National Socialism – Catalogue of the Munich Documentation Centre for the History of National Socialism* (bookstore edition) (Munich: Verlag C.H. Beck oHG, 2015)

36. The Editors of Encyclopaedia Britannica, Encyclopaedia Britannica, "Andrej Hlinka Slovak Patriot," http://www.britannica.com/EBchecked/topic/268250/Andrej-Hlinka (2015)

37. Hannah Rothschild, *The Baroness: The Search for Nica, the Rebellious Rothschild,* (New York: Knopf, 2013), (p105)

38. "Over all summits" first line from Wanderers Nachtlied II (Wanderer's Night Song II)

39. Father Brown was an American Catholic priest also studying at the University that summer.

40. Burghard Ciesla, Mathias Judt, *Technology Transfer out of Germany after 1945 (Business and Economics)*, (London: Rutledge, May 13, 2013) (p71)

41. The Editors of Encyclopaedia Britannica, Encyclopaedia Britannica, "Béla Imrédy, Premier of Hungary," http://www.britannica.com/biography/Bela-Imredy (2015)

42. The Editors of Encyclopaedia Britannica, Encyclopaedia Britannica, "Spanish Civil War," http://www.britannica.com/event/Spanish-Civil-War (2015)

43. International Herald Tribune, New York Herald Tribune, European Edition, "1939: Fascist Italy Issues Book Ban," August 15, 1939 http://iht-retrospective.blogs.nytimes.com/2014/08/14/1939-fascist-italy-issues-book-ban/?_r=0 (2015)

44. The Editors of Encyclopaedia Britannica, Encyclopaedia Britannica, "Kurt Eisner, German journalist and statesman," http://www.britannica.com/biography/Kurt-Eisner(2015)

45. The Editors of Encyclopaedia Britannica, Encyclopaedia Britannica, "German-Soviet Nonaggression Pact – Germany – Union of Soviet Socialist Republics (1939)," http://www.britannica.com/event/German-Soviet-Nonaggression-Pact (2015)

46. Mark Fielder, BBC History, "Countdown to World War Two: Wednesday 30 August 1939" http://www.bbc.co.uk/history/worldwars/wwtwo/countdown_390830_wed_01.shtml (2015)

47. Roger Manvell, Heinrich Fraenkel, *Heinrich Himmler: The SS, Gestapo, His Life and Career,*(Skyhorse Publishing Inc., 2007) (p 76)

48. Die Welt, Geschichte 1. September 1939, "Seit 5.45 Uhr wird jetzt zurückgeschossen!" http://www.welt.de/geschichte/zweiter-weltkrieg/

article131718545/Seit-5-45-Uhr-wird-jetzt-zurueckgeschossen.html (2015)

49. John Graham Royde-Smith, Encyclopaedia Britannica, "World War ii – 1939 – 1945," http://www.britannica.com/event/World-War-II#ref511786 (2015)

50. Ibid

51. Ibid

52. Gavriel D. Rosenfeld, *Munich and Memory: Architecture, Monuments, and the Legacy of the Third Reich* (University of California Press, 2000) , (p 132)

53. Comedian and actor who was close to the Nazi party.

54. Jewish Virtual Library, "The Holocaust: Jews in Germany Pre-World War II (January 22-23, 1934)," https://www.jewishvirtuallibrary.org/jsource/Holocaust/manchester.html (2015)

55. Yale Law School, Lillian Goldman Low Library, in memory of Sol Goldman, "Judgement: Streicher," http://avalon.law.yale.edu/imt/judstrei.asp (2015)

56. Jewish Virtual Library, "Dachau Concentration Camp: History & Overview," https://www.jewishvirtuallibrary.org/jsource/Holocaust/dachau.html (2015)

57. National 4th Infantry (IVY) Division Association – Supporting the Veterans, Soldiers and Friends of the 4th Infantry Division Since 1919, www.4thinfantry.org (2015)

58. The Rosary is a set of prayers with prescribed meditations on events from the life of Christ and his mother. Beads can be used to keep track of the numbers, but are not necessary.

59. "Blessings in Disguise Memoir of Faith, Hope and Love. David Joseph LaFia, MD

60. Peiper was a member of the "Leibstandarte – SS Adolf Hitler" an SS outfit established in 1933. The SS was an elite group, separate from the army. The SS was a volunteer army whose soldiers swore loyalty to Adolf Hitler rather than to their country, as did the Wehrmacht soldiers. Peiper and others served jail time for this massacre. From the Jewish Virtual Library, "Massacre at Malmédy: War Crimes Trial (May 12 – July 16, 1946)," https://www.jewishvirtuallibrary.org/jsource/ww2/malmedy2.html (2015)

61. Ken White, IMCOM-Europe Public Affairs Office, "Malmédy Survivor Recalls Massacre," December 21, 2007, http://www.army.mil/article/6726/MalmAfAdy_Survivor_Recalls_Massacre/ (2015)

62. Danny S. Parker. *Fatal Crossroads: The Untold Story of the Malmedy Massacre at the Battle of the Bulge.* (Da Capo Press, First Trade Paper edition, 2012)

63. Bradley A. Thayer. *Darwin and International Relations: On the Evolutionary Origins of War and Ethnic Conflict.* (Lexington: University Press of Kentucky, 2004)

64. The National WWII Museum, New Orleans, "After the Camps: Guests of the Third Reich American POWs in Europe" http://www.guestsofthethirdreich.org/ home/ (2015)

65. Cornell University Law School, "Geneva Conventions," https://www.law. cornell.edu/wex/geneva_conventions (2015)

66. Steve Inskeep, "'Soldiers and Slaves' Details Saga of Jewish POWs," NPR Books. May 30, 2005 http://www.npr.org/templates/story/story.php?storyId=4672288 (2015)

67. Pegasus Archive, "Stalag XIIA," http://www.pegasusarchive.org/pow/cSt_12A_ History1.htm (2015)

68. The National WWII Museum, New Orleans, "After the Camps: Guests of the Third Reich American POWs in Europe," http://www.guestsofthethirdreich.org/ home/ (2015)

69. Jabo is an abbreviation for Jäger-Bomber, or fighter-bomber – American planes which had 2 bombs and machine guns.

70. Bob Babcock, 4IDA President, Historian and Archivist, "4th Infantry Division Archives."

71. Dave Wilton, "1904 Words," (January 2012) http://www.wordorigins.org/ index.php/site/comments/1904_words/ (2015)

72. In August 2015, early notes of a transcription in 1984 of the WWII diary were found in the bottom of George's desk.

73. Thomas M. Leonard, *Encyclopedia of the Developing World*, (Psychology Press, 2005, Business and Economics) (p361)

74. "Indian Army Victoria Cross Holders (awarded during the Second World War) (1939-1945)" http://www.victoriacross.org.uk/ccww2ina.htm (2015)

75. Philip B. Calkins, Encyclopaedia Britannica, "India" http://www.britannica. com/place/India/History#ref486438 (2015)

76. The Editors of Encyclopaedia Britannica, Encyclopaedia Britannica, "Subhas

Chandra Bose, Indian Military leader," http://www.britannica.com/biography/ Subhas-Chandra-Bose (2015)

77. Mike Thomson, BBC News, "Hitler's secret Indian Army," Thursday 23 September 2004, http://news.bbc.co.uk/2/hi/europe/3684288.stm (2015)

78. Ibid

79. Ibid

80. Ibid

81. Royal Institute of International Affairs, *Chronology and Index of the Second World War, 1938 – 45,* (Information Today, March 14, 1990)

82. United Nations, "The History of the United Nations, Declaration by United Nations," http://www.un.org/en/aboutun/history/declaration.shtml (2015)

83. United Nations, "The Atlantic Charter," http://www.un.org/en/aboutun/ history/atlantic_charter.shtml (2015)

84. Ibid

85. United Nations, "History of the United Nations," http://www.un.org/en/ aboutun/history/ (2015)

86. The Editors of Encyclopaedia Britannica, Encyclopaedia Britannica, "Trench warfare," http://www.britannica.com/topic/trench-warfare (2015)

87. United Nations, "Declaration by United Nations," http://www.un.org/en/ aboutun/history/declaration.shtml (2015)

88. The Editors of Encyclopaedia Britannica, Encyclopaedia Britannica, "Waldenses Religious Movement," http://www.britannica.com/topic/Waldenses (2015)

89. "Historic Valdese North Carolina," http://townofvaldese.com/pages/heritage/

90. Dollar Times, http://www.dollartimes.com/inflation/inflation. php?amount=6&year=1945 (2015)

91. The History Learning Site, "The bombing of Coventry in 1940, " http://www. historylearningsite.co.uk/world-war-two/world-war-two-in-western-europe/ britains-home-front-in-world-war-two/the-bombing-of-coventry-in-1940/ (2015)

92. Thomas Mallon, "Rocket Man the complex orbits of Wernher von Braun," The New Yorker October 22, 2007 http://www.newyorker.com/ magazine/2007/10/22/rocket-man (2015)

93. This Day in History World War II 1942, "Germany conducts first successful

V-2 rocket test," http://www.history.com/this-day-in-history/germany-conducts-first-successful-v-2-rocket-test (2015)

94. Ibid

95. World War II History Info, "North Africa: Introduction to the North African Campaign," http://www.worldwar2history.info/North-Africa/ (2015)

96. Pegasus Archive, "Stalag XIIA," http://www.pegasusarchive.org/pow/cSt_12A_History1.htm (2015)

97. Ibid

98. John Graham Royde-Smith, Encyclopaedia Britannica, "WWII 1939-1945," http://www.britannica.com/EBchecked/topic/648813/World-War-II/53600/The-German-collapse-spring-1945 (2015)

99. Pegasus Archive, "Stalag XIIA," http://www.pegasusarchive.org/pow/cSt_12A_History1.htm (2015)

100. The National WWII Museum, New Orleans, "After the Camps: Guests of the Third Reich American POWs in Europe" http://www.guestsofthethirdreich.org/home/ (2015)

101. "The Cigarette Camps, the U.S. Army Camps in the Le Havre Area," http://www.skylighters.org/special/cigcamps/cigintro.html (2015)

102. Ibid

103. "Blessings in Disguise: Memoir of Faith, Hope and Love" David Joseph LaFia, M.D.

104. "A German-American Chronology," http://maxkade.iupui.edu/adams/chrono.html (2015)

105. The Evening Independent, "Fritz Kuhn, Former Bund Chief, Ordered Back to Germany" September 7, 1945 https://news.google.com/

106. Robert D. McFadden, The New York Times, "David Greenglass, the Brother who Doomed Ethel Rosenberg, Dies at 92," October 14, 2014 http://www.nytimes.com/2014/10/15/us/david-greenglass-spy-who-helped-seal-the-rosenbergs-doom-dies-at-92.html?_r=0 (2015)

107. This Day In History, "1950 – Klaus Fuchs arrested for passing atomic bomb information to Soviets," http://www.history.com/this-day-in-history/klaus-fuchs-arrested-for-passing-atomic-bomb-information-to-soviets (2015)

108. U.S. Department of State, Office of the Historian, "Milestones: 1945-1952 –

Marshall Plan, 1948," https://history.state.gov/milestones/1945-1952/marshall-plan (2015)

109. Katharina von Kellenbach, *The Mark of Cain: Guilt and Denial in the Post-War Lives of Nazi Perpetrators* (Oxford University Press, June 25, 2013)

110. Arieh J. Kochavi, *Prelude to Nuremberg: Allied War Crimes Policy and the Question of Punishment,* (The University of North Carolina Press, November 30, 2005)

111. Tom Fox, Inquirer Editorial Board, "Trip to Herbrechtingen Returning the Flag was Something to Sing About," April 20, 1986. http://articles.philly.com/1986-04-20/news/26077127_1_banner-war-story-war-souvenir (2015)

112. Megan McDonough, The Washington Post, "Franz M. and Margaret F. Oppenheimer, a lawyer and a teacher, die at 95 and 93" http://www.washingtonpost.com/local/obituaries/franz-m-and-margaret-f-oppenheimer-a-lawyer-and-a-teacher-die-at-95-and-93/2014/12/17/7a7c6a04-860b-11e4-9534-f79a23c40e6c_story.html (2015)

113. New York Times, "J.J. Petuchowski, 66, A Rabbi and Professor," November 15, 1991 http://www.nytimes.com/1991/11/15/obituaries/j-j-petuchowski-66-a-rabbi-and-professor.html (2015)

114. Saint Joseph's University Magazine Fall 2014, p.28

115. "A War Story" by Kristin A. Graham. SJU Magazine, St Joseph's University, Fall 2014

116. German American Heritage Foundation of the USA, http://gahmusa.org/ (2015)

About the Author

LISA BEICHL IS THE YOUNGEST OF GEORGE and Isabella Beichl's four daughters. Professionally she focuses on international health insurance development, with a strong interest in the working poor and has been able to travel the world in this role. She leads the development of global evidence based tools and consulting for employers, governments and other organizations to target the most relevant health and well-being risks (www.transparent-borders.com). Her roots in a Jesuit education include a BA degree from Loyola College in Maryland and an MBA degree in finance from St. Joseph's University. Lisa has published articles on the impact of health insurance in international settings, global employee productivity as it relates to health and well-being, and micro-health insurance. She maintains a strong interest in balancing public and private sector perspectives to ensure the long-term viability of quality programs. She is still working on mastering the bagpipes.

CPSIA information can be obtained at www.ICGtesting.com
Printed in the USA
BVOW11s0940311015

425045BV00001B/1/P